What Others are Saying About this Book

"*Your Career, Your Way!* is a great tool for women to navigate through the business world. Lisa Quast has created a practical format any career woman can use to create a strategy for success. She gets right to the bottom line of what you need to do to be successful. This book is invaluable coming from a woman who has successfully climbed the corporate ladder. Lisa, thank you so much for such a worthwhile contribution."

– Hellen Davis
Author, The 21 Laws of Influence

"This book gives women the business formula for a successful career. Anyone who wants their career – their way, can utilize these strategies to make their dream a reality."

– Carolyn Gross
Author, Staying Calm in the Midst of Chaos

"Written in a crisp, no-nonsense style, the premise of *Your Career, Your Way!* is that women should view their talents and skills as competitive products to be offered carefully to potential employers. Strategic planning was developed to help businesses position themselves competitively. Using *Your Career, Your Way!*, the reader can do the same for themselves, following ten crucial steps, from assessing assets and liabilities to goal setting and finally to success. This is a working book, meant to be written in, digested, and taken seriously as a basis for developing a professional lifestyle. The book is sprinkled liberally with inspirational quotes from famous women, quotes that set the stage for the reader's identification of professional strengths, weaknesses, opportunities, and threats. Examples are given for each exercise, followed by templates for the reader to complete and supplemental information on finding a mentor, selecting a coach, goal-setting, evaluating accomplishments, and celebrating success. *Your Career, Your Way!* would be an excellent gift for any woman developing a professional career."

– ForeWord CLARION Reviews

"If you want to get ahead in the business world, just read the step-by-step instructions provided in Lisa Quast's first book. Any woman who aspires to climb the corporate ladder would find much useful information in this slim volume."

– The Odessa Record

"*Your Career, Your Way!* is an invaluable guidebook for any woman wanting to advance their career and achieve their aspirations."

– Charles Hasse
President, Washington Education Association

"Your Career, Your Way! should be the reference guide for all women who want to advance in their careers! As a professional trainer, I was amazed at how easily the reader is able to advance through the chapters, completing the exercises and developing their very own personal career strategic plan. It's an amazingly helpful book and should be on the desks of women around the world."

– Al Patey
President, Paradigm Training

"Your Career, Your Way! provides highly personalized tools required to assess ones individual strengths, weaknesses and ambitions. This information is then converted into a strategic plan which will lead that individual to a life of success and satisfaction. The book's process is a powerful approach toward achieving the ultimate goal in life, namely happiness and contentment. I highly recommend this masterpiece since it contains an amazing compilation of facts and processes that will guide the serious reader to 'being the best one is capable of becoming'".

– F. David Rollo M.D., PhD., FACC, FACNP
President, Cell>Point

"Your Career, Your Way!" is an essential career roadmap that provides a realistic, practical approach to help you navigate to your next position. Lisa Quast has provided wonderful landmarks for those who have already started down the path, and an easy-to-follow journal for those who want to begin the journey. The book is a wonderful antidote to the old saying, 'If you don't know where you're going, you'll probably end up someplace else'"!

– Louise A. Kapustka
Director, Executive MBA Program
University of Washington Business School

"This book really enables people to think about their personal and professional development in practical business terms. With her structured step by step approach and speaking from her rich experience in business and as a coach, Lisa provides self-confidence to anyone wanting to take a next step in their careers, but not being sure yet on how best to do that."

– Carla Mahieu
Senior Vice President Executive Staffing & Talent Management
Philips International

"I wish this book had been written sooner! Your Career, Your Way! easily and simply demonstrates how to apply some of the fundamental tools of business (S.W.O.T. analysis, listening to your customers, evaluating your competitors, 'SMART' goals, etc.) to yourself and take your career to the next level. Every woman who wants to advance in her career should read this book!"

– Rebecca Baker
Chief Marketing Officer of Alvarez & Marsal Holdings, LLC

"One of the greatest challenges women face either entering the business world or advancing their business careers is having a personal and strategic plan. Two questions that often come up, "how do I begin and what are my options? Lisa Quast's book, "Your Career, Your Way!" is designed to help women make informed decisions on how to jump start their careers and what steps they can take to achieve personal fulfillment. Through Lisa's successful business experience, she has provided women with business tools and know how to execute and succeed in their chosen career goals."

– Ellen Moos
Owner and Creative Director, Silver Fox Productions

"Many times we think of a career woman only as a woman in the business world climbing the corporate ladder. After reading this book I realized the importance of organizing my ideas and goals for the future as an educator. This organization is needed as a teacher, nurse, or any college student getting ready to enter the 'real world' of work."

– Cindy Remme
Clinical Assistant Professor, Teacher and Teacher Education,
University of Arizona

"Lisa Quast has offered many working women (and, as far as I'm concerned, men!) an extremely useful guide to planning their careers and lives. Her way of providing a thinking framework for people to get to grips with who they are and where they want to go is both refreshing and practical."

– Tjerk Hooghiemstra
Corporate HRM, Philips International

"Look out men in the world because women have a new champion, mentor and leader. With the reading of her book, 'Your Career, Your Way!', women will have a leg up on their competition."

– Robert Boyd
President, Orca Creative Group

"Businessmen, you better be 'checking your six' because Lisa Quast is a serious Top Gun. This amazing book is a perfect flight plan for women looking to add thrust to their career. A must read for women looking to advance their careers."

– Rob "Waldo" Waldman
Former Fighter Pilot, Keynote Speaker and Author

Your Career, Your Way!

Personal Strategies to Achieve Your Career Aspirations

BY LISA QUAST

Your Career, Your Way!
LISA QUAST

Editor: Wingspan Press
Cover Design: Silver Fox Productions
Cover Photography: Doug Ogle Photography
Interior Design & Production: Silver Fox Productions

Career Woman Inc.	Silver Fox Productions	Wingspan Press
www.careerwomaninc.com	www.silverfoxprod.com	www.wingspanpress.com

Library of Congress Cataloging-in-Publication Data

Quast, Lisa.

   Your career, your way : personal strategies to achieve your career aspirations / by Lisa Quast. – 1s t edition

   p. cm.

   ISBN 978-1-59594-042-1 (alk. paper)

   1. Vocational guidance for women. 2. Career development. I. Title.

HF5382.6.Q37 2006

650.14082–dc22

2006012619

Printed and bound in the United States of America

Dedication

Your Career, Your Way! is dedicated to all women who do not want to trust their job satisfaction and career advancement to luck or fate. It is designed for women who want to advance their career, their way and achieve their career aspirations on their terms.

I believe women's leadership potential, business acumen, level-headedness and emotional maturity remains largely untapped in the business world. Women who are willing to make the effort and commit themselves to a plan of action will open the doors of opportunity and achieve the success and personal fulfillment they desire. I dedicate this book to all these women!

Foreword

LISA QUAST: This book was truly written from the heart. It was written because of my own experiences and the excitement I feel when I've accomplished more than anyone else thought was possible. I've learned that it's o.k. to reach for the sky; that it's o.k. to take control of my career and my life. I've learned that it's o.k. to be female, ambitious and successful.

Why focus on helping women? Quite simply – women represent the future. According to the U.S. Department of Labor, Bureau of Labor Statistics, women currently represent 47 percent of the total U.S. labor force and will account for 55 percent of the increase in total labor force growth from 2002–2012. Women represent what will be the most exciting and incremental breakthrough in the world of business: assuming their hard won place beside their male counterparts.

Women currently have greater success than men in attending postsecondary education. Women also have higher aspirations than men while in school; they are more likely to enroll in college immediately after graduation from high school, and complete degrees at higher rates than men. Further, more than half of all bachelor's and master's degrees are awarded to women. (Trends in Educational Equality of Girls and Women – U.S. Department of Education)

Too often, as women, we experience little encouragement to reach for our dreams or attempt the impossible. We may start as young girls who think we can take on the world and do or be anything we want, but somewhere along the way things change and we lose our resolve.

My personal goal in writing this book is to provide women with an easy-to-follow plan and the encouragement necessary to help them achieve their career aspirations. Writing this book and knowing the information in it can positively change women's lives fuels my resolve to help more women rediscover their wings and take flight.

After reading this book, I sincerely hope you will find that my passion for helping other women achieve their dreams is contagious. Use your knowledge and experience in creating and implementing your personal strategic plan to help other women. Reach out and offer to help others as you move up the career ladder – become a mentor and help another woman realize her dreams and aspirations.

Table of Contents

Introduction

"Life is change. Growth is optional. Choose wisely."
— Karen Kaiser Clark

L et's face it – life isn't easy and some days, it sure doesn't feel very fair. How many of us spent time in school never doubting that our education and training were preparing us for successful careers? How many of us later discovered we had not been prepared to navigate the continual changes in the workplace? I don't know about you, but when I was in school, no one taught me the skills or an approach to systematically achieve my career goals and aspirations. The popular notion was to join a company, go with the flow and hope that somebody, some day, would recognize my skills, abilities and potential and pluck me from the masses to help me rise to business stardom. Yeah, right. Has this happened to you? It doesn't happen for most of us.

Have you ever found yourself participating on projects but not given opportunities to lead those projects? Have you ever been assigned menial tasks – tasks that might be considered grunt work as opposed to higher profile work that could bring individual recognition and allow for growth in your skills and abilities? Have you ever competed for a position not only with your co-workers, but also with people located throughout the world? This was increasingly becoming my experience, and it concerned me.

As a college student I felt that I could achieve anything and I graduated believing I could take on the world. Once I became immersed in the business world, the reality of my situation became painfully clear. I was functioning in a world where my potential was not being fully realized. I often felt under utilized and under appreciated. I realized I had been waiting for others to recognize my great work; I had been waiting for others to see my potential. I had been waiting for others to promote me to higher challenges. In essence, I felt a little like a cork bobbing in a stream and going wherever the current took me instead of taking control of my own career and steering myself to destinations of my choice.

I decided that something had to change. I had two choices: either I could remain a powerless passenger on a road to career obscurity or I could identify and take specific actions that would allow me to manage my career my way. I didn't want to just survive in my career. I wanted to *thrive* in my career.

While working one day on a strategic plan for a new product, I experienced an epiphany. For years, I had written strategic plans that created roadmaps for products and businesses to be successful in the marketplace. Why couldn't I write my very own personal strategic plan, using myself as the product? What could I achieve if I applied a business concept to myself?

> *"The best way to predict your future is to create it."*
> – Anonymous

I decided to treat my career as a business and myself as a competitive product. I created a strategic plan to manage my career and continually upgrade my product in order to achieve a competitive advantage. I systematically evaluated my assets, liabilities, and competition and then determined my differentiators. Because I had never before looked at myself as a product or taken this kind of proactive approach with my career, I found my self-evaluation to be an eye-opening experience.

What I found when I took control of my career is that I received promotions, assignments giving me greater visibility, more money, appreciation from management, respect and recognition from colleagues, and new job offers. I ended up feeling great about myself and what I was accomplishing! All of this resulted from my knowing what I wanted and having a strategic plan detailing how I was going to achieve it! *I* was now in control.

From my experience, I identified 10 key strategic essentials any woman can follow or use in creating a personal strategic plan and achieving their career aspirations. These strategic essentials can be applied by women of any age, in any type of business, large or small, public, private or government operated, and located anywhere in the world. They are the following:

1. **Review your Assets and Liabilities:** Remind yourself that you are valuable and that you possess strengths. Define yourself as a competitive product. Challenge yourself by facing any weaknesses and commit yourself to systematic improvement and upgrades.

2. **Determine your Differentiators:** Just as products have strengths that set them apart, so do people. A differentiator is a competitive advantage. Identify those things that you do better than other people. Your distinctive strengths are what others perceive your value to be.

3. **Obtain Customer Feedback:** Perception is reality. Seek to understand the perception others (i.e. friends, family and colleagues) have of you. With this knowledge you can be confident of your assessment of your assets, liabilities and differentiators. If you find that a change needs to be made, you are then in a better position to focus your time and efforts to make this happen.

4. **Identify and Evaluate your Competitors:** Competition is a fact of life. Simply doing your job and hoping for the best is not enough. You need to compete for what you want. Competition and what you can learn from it should be viewed positively and embraced. Strive to be your best by understanding yourself and your competitors.

5. **Determine your Goals:** Goals reflect what you want to accomplish to improve yourself. They are your targets, both short-term and long-term. Goal setting will lead you to a greater sense of commitment and motivation as you pursue your aspirations.

6. **Create your Strategic Plan:** Like using a roadmap to arrive at a destination, having a clear plan in place helps assure you achieve your aspirations in the shortest period of time and in the most efficient manner. A plan provides a clear sense of direction and defines the components that will support the achievement of your aspirations. Clarify your aspirations by building a personal strategic plan that will help lead you to success.

7. **Implement your Strategic Plan:** Strategic plans, like ideas, are effective only if you implement them. You alone are accountable for your success or failure – you are your own CEO. You must combine the determination to succeed with a commitment to prepare yourself to succeed. Don't just survive life; live it to its fullest.

8. **Check your Progress:** Having and implementing a strategic plan requires that you review and demonstrate progress in order to take corrective action. Make immediate corrections to unproductive or unsuccessful plans as soon as they become apparent. Do not procrastinate!

9. **Stay Focused:** Tenacity, courage and commitment are essential to achieving your aspirations. Staying focused is up to you. Only you can achieve your dreams. Focus on the positive, but be prepared to overcome obstacles. Be aware that all plans, at some point, may need to be modified.

10. **Celebrate and Reward Incremental Achievements:** Giving yourself encouragement and rewards will provide motivation and pleasure as you continue achieving your goals. You cannot count on others to shine a spotlight on you. You must be your own coach / manager.

"The future belongs to those who believe in the beauty of their dreams."
– Eleanor Roosevelt

As you read this book, some of you will be saying to yourself, "I'm not sure what my career aspiration is right now." That's o.k. You may be just graduating from college and entering the workplace for the first time or returning to work after a long absence and your aspiration right now is simply to find a job. You may have a job that you enjoy and your aspiration may be to continually improve yourself. My recommendation in all cases (whether you have a defined aspiration or not) is to begin by identifying what is important to you. Then, be courageous in all the things you do and never stop believing in yourself. You only have one life to live so find your passion! Love what you do and do what you love.

Over the next ten chapters, using the help of two fictional characters (Cheryl and Mackenzie), I will share techniques that will enable you to take control of your career and achieve your aspirations. As you begin this journey, I can tell you that while I believe it can change your life, it will not always be easy. Few things worth doing are easily done. Often it is hard work, effort and endurance that bring the greatest rewards of self-awareness and understanding, and of growth and personal satisfaction. And, of course, career advancement.

While I chose to use Cheryl, age 39, and Mackenzie, age 27, for the examples, you can use the techniques and exercises in this book no matter what your age. I have coached women who have had tremendous success applying these concepts whether they were 20 years old or 50 years old. We can all keep learning and growing at any age!

To get the most benefit from this book, I recommend you find a quiet location to relax and enjoy reading it cover-to-cover in one or two sittings. Then, go back to each chapter and work through the exercises over a period of several weeks. This approach will help provide you with a thorough understanding of the work you will need to complete before you create your personal strategic plan.

Each chapter and its associated exercises are interrelated. Each was written to be challenging, yet easy to complete. Do not get discouraged – you are worth the effort! To assist you in the exercises, all templates are available electronically to download. Just go to the website, **www.careerwomaninc.com** and from the Home Page, click on "**Resources**" – then look for this book and you may download the templates after you enter the password, "**Athena**".

There are many special people I would like to acknowledge for their incredible help and support while I wrote this book. Thank you to: Paul Murdoch for his critical reviews and his uncanny ability to always be honest with his feedback; Sonja Rothfuss, Glenda Stilwell and Deanna Allen for amazingly comprehensive edits and improvement suggestions throughout the process; Ellen Moos, Staci Carlson, Maria Ehsan, Kristin Cusolito, Susan Fleenor and Amy Guistino for wonderful, varying perspectives of women in different industries and at different stages in their careers; all of the hand-picked women test-readers, from ages 18 to 68 – you know who you are; and my parents, sister and husband's family for their positive support and suggestions. And finally, thank you to my husband, my #1 fan, for all your love and encouragement. You are my soul mate and I love you.

In writing this book, my goal is to help women around the world succeed in the workplace and achieve their career aspirations by proactively creating and implementing their own personal strategic plan.

Queen Margreth II of Denmark once remarked, "I have always had a dread of becoming a passenger in life." The choice is yours to manage *your* career, *your* way. I look forward to guiding you on your journey.

So, let's get started.

– Lisa Quast, January 2007

CHAPTER 1:
Review your Assets and Liabilities

"One only gets to the top rung on the ladder by steadily climbing up one at a time, and suddenly all sorts of powers, all sorts of abilities which you thought never belonged to you – suddenly become within your own possibility and you think, 'Well, I'll have a go, too.'"

— Margaret Thatcher

When you are shopping for yourself or your family and look at all the products from which you can choose, in your mind, you perform comparisons of the products. You judge the products by their strengths and weaknesses to determine which ones best fit your needs. When a company is selling a product, the goal is not to only offer a great product, but also promote the strengths of their product that best meet the needs of customers. Hopefully, the product will be perceived as superior to competitive products and will exceed the customers' expectations in value and usefulness.

Picture yourself, if you will, as a competitive product. A company hires you for a specific function with the expectation that you will meet a specific need. The level at which you perform your job and the quality of the results influence your value and importance as an employee. How you perform is totally within your control to affect and manage. You can perform at a minimum level to just meet the need or you can work to exceed expectations and anticipate new needs.

Like a product with strengths and weaknesses, each of us possesses strengths and weaknesses. In this chapter you will be asked to complete an inventory designed to identify your personal assets and liabilities. This is the first step in determining how best to market yourself as a competitive product.

In the context of this book, a personal strength is an asset. Having strong orga-
nizational skills, intelligence, tenacity and self-confidence are examples of personal
strengths. In the context of this book, a personal weakness is a liability or an area
of opportunity for growth. Being inflexible, disorganized, having a lack of skills or
difficulty communicating ideas are examples of personal weaknesses. Knowing your
personal assets and liabilities will be to your advantage.

Throughout this book I will use the help of two fictional characters, Cheryl
and Mackenzie, to demonstrate the various exercises. Cheryl is 39 years old, married
to Bob, with two sons, ages 10 and 12. She began working during high school at a
small, local clothing store and kept working to help put her husband through college.
Cheryl took time out of her career to have children and went back to work at age 37.
She currently works as an administrative assistant to a clothing buyer and aspires to
become a clothing buyer herself.

Mackenzie is 27 years old, single with no children. Working part-time during
college to pay her tuition and expenses, she earned a four-year college degree in
communications. She currently works as an associate marketing manager at a
technology company and aspires to become the vice president of marketing, but isn't
sure how to go about achieving this goal.

The first assignment for Cheryl and Mackenzie is to establish a baseline of self-
awareness of their assets and liabilities. Read how they work through the exercise to
determine their assets and liabilities.

It's the end of the day; Cheryl and her family have finished dinner and cleaned
up the kitchen. Her children are upstairs working on their homework and Bob is in
the living room watching the news on TV. Cheryl makes herself a cup of tea, grabs
a notepad and pen and sits down at the kitchen table to brainstorm her assets and
liabilities. She divides the first sheet of paper in half and writes Assets on the top left
side, and Liabilities on the top right side. Cheryl understands that the trick to this
exercise is to write down all her thoughts as quickly as possible, knowing there are no
wrong answers.

Cheryl thinks about various positive comments she has received from co-workers
and from her manager during performance appraisals and jots down notes. She
remembers how often co-workers have told her she is the most organized, hardest
working individual they have ever met. She smiles, reflecting on her manager's
compliments on her willingness to go the extra mile to meet critical deadlines.

Cheryl also thinks about the areas she would like to improve. Because she has
taken time out of her career for children and has been back in the workforce only two

years, Cheryl is still feeling a little intimidated in certain situations. She realizes that her lack of confidence could be holding her back. She also realizes this is probably why she often keeps quiet during staff meetings, even when she believes she has good ideas. Within about 30 minutes, Cheryl has a fairly complete list of her assets and liabilities.

Cheryl's Assets and Liabilities:

ASSETS	LIABILITIES
• Organized • Hard worker • Supportive • Accountable • Professional appearance • Good listener • Positive attitude	• Lacks some confidence in certain situations • Not outspoken • Needs more experience in a leadership role

Cheryl is amazed. Viewing the list as if she's a competitive product, suddenly, this isn't just a list of words. Her list of attributes affirms the valuable contribution she provides at work each day. And the more she thinks about her assets, the more she realizes how many people depend on her and view her as a key member and contributor to the company.

In looking at her liabilities, Cheryl realizes that these are definitely areas in which she could work to improve. And, if she could improve in these areas, it might further enhance her future opportunities.

Now let's check in with Mackenzie. It's late Saturday morning and Mackenzie heads to her favorite coffee shop. She sits down in the corner table with her notepad and pen and, while sipping her latte, completes her list. In less than 10 minutes, she is done.

Mackenzie's first Assets and Liabilities List:

ASSETS	LIABILITIES
• Creative	• Uncomfortable speaking before large groups
• Expressive	• Could be more organized
• Goal oriented	• Tends to take on too many projects
• Decisive	• Poor listener
	• Sometimes too casual in appearance
	• Procrastinates
	• Bad hair
	• Overweight

Glancing up from her list, Mackenzie sees her best friend Alicia walk in the door. After buying a mocha, she joins Mackenzie. Mackenzie decides to share her brainstorming exercise and the two look over the list together. "Mackenzie, I can't believe you said you have bad hair and are overweight!" says Alicia. "You're kidding, right? How can you say that you're overweight? And what's wrong with your hair? I'd love to have your hair! Don't be overly critical of yourself." Mackenzie laughs, and then crosses both comments off her liabilities list.

"You seem to focus more on your liabilities than your assets," Alicia notices. "Aren't you the one with the aspiration of becoming the vice president of marketing? You should add confident and a risk-taker to your list of assets." With those two items added to her assets category, Mackenzie reviews her updated list:

Mackenzie's updated Assets and Liabilities List:

ASSETS	LIABILITIES
• Creative	• Uncomfortable speaking before large groups
• Expressive	• Could be more organized
• Goal oriented	• Tends to take on too many projects
• Decisive	• Poor listener
• Confident	• Sometimes too casual in appearance
• Risk-taker	• Procrastinates

Mackenzie feels self-doubt as she reads what she has written about herself. "If this is how I view myself as a product, I wonder if this is how other people at work view me? How many times have I gone into the office wearing jeans and a sweater instead of a business suit? How many times have I taken on projects and failed to complete them on time? Am I viewed as being on the fast track for promotion or as just another employee? How do others perceive me as a product?"

Now that I've shared the experiences of Cheryl and Mackenzie, let's move the focus to you. It's time for you to create your own personal assets and liabilities list. On the following page is a template you can use to complete this exercise. In the Assets section, brainstorm your strengths. In the Liabilities section, brainstorm your weaknesses or areas of opportunity for growth.

One quick reminder though, it's easier to complete the exercises in this book *after* you have read the book once from cover to cover. After reading the book, come back to each exercise, work through them and they will have more meaning for you.

Here are some helpful hints to follow as you complete this exercise:

- Choose a location that is comfortable for you to work in before you begin.
- Approach this exercise with a fresh mindset; clear your mind, be relaxed and refreshed before you start. If you've had a bad day, this is definitely not the time to complete this exercise.
- Make some photocopies of the page before you begin, or download the templates from the website. *(See page 105 for more information.)* You can use these as scratch paper while you brainstorm and jot down your thoughts.
- Write down your thoughts as quickly as possible.
- Remember, there are no wrong answers.
- Avoid the tendency to be overly critical of yourself in the Liabilities category.
- View yourself as a competitive product and have some fun creating your list!

_____'s *List of Assets and Liabilities:*

ASSETS	LIABILITIES
• _____	• _____
_____	_____
• _____	• _____
_____	_____
• _____	• _____
_____	_____
• _____	• _____
_____	_____
• _____	• _____
_____	_____
• _____	• _____
_____	_____
• _____	• _____
_____	_____

Congratulations on finishing your list! By understanding and developing confidence in your assets, you will learn to depend on them as you face challenges. Reminding yourself of your best qualities will increase your confidence and your ability to project a positive, can-do attitude. As Martha Washington so eloquently once said, "The greater part of our happiness or misery depends on our dispositions and not our circumstances." Be proud of your assets and celebrate them!

You've just finished the important first step in the creation of your very own personal strategic plan. As you work through this book, it's important to understand that you shouldn't focus on your liabilities as a barrier, you should commit yourself to making systematic improvements or learning new skills that will move your liabilities into the assets category. I'll help you do just that throughout this book. Also, don't let your weaknesses dictate your self worth. These are areas of opportunity. Don't worry that you have liabilities, everyone does and no one is perfect. As one smart woman once said, "Don't get your knickers in a knot. Nothing is solved and it just makes you walk funny."

Believe in yourself! The process of magnifying your assets and eliminating your liabilities will translate into improved work performance and positively impact the perception others have of you.

Remember, you are a competitive product. Be assertive as you market yourself against your competitors. Be willing to stretch yourself by taking calculated risks and becoming an even better product than you are right now. Be determined to fully participate in life and steer your career in the direction *you* choose.

"The secret of getting ahead is getting started."
– Sally Berger

CHAPTER 1:

Strategic Essential

Review Your Assets and Liabilities: *Remind yourself that you are valuable and that you possess strengths. Define yourself as a competitive product. Challenge yourself by facing any weaknesses and commit yourself to systematic improvement and upgrades.*

CHAPTER 2:
Determine your Differentiators

"As is our confidence, so is our capacity."

— William Hazlitt

Each day we are faced with the decision of selecting and purchasing products we will use in our lives. With countless products available to us, we learn to recognize distinctive assets in certain products that lead us to trust in their performance and return to them. Whether it's laundry detergent getting the whites whiter, wanting to own a BMW because it's the "ultimate driving machine", or Nike encouraging us to Just Do It™, we evaluate our choices and determine whether these products have assets that set them apart. Those assets are known as the product differentiators, and product differentiators result in competitive advantages.

Just like products, people have distinctive assets too, which can be the differentiators that set one apart from the others. For example, you are at a job interview and you are asked the following questions: "Why should I hire you for this position? What makes you different from all the other candidates I've interviewed?" In order to even be considered for the job, you need to have a thoughtful, succinct answer that demonstrates your key differentiators. What would you say?

Another example is your resume. Resumés are used to persuade potential employers to hire you over other candidates because you are not only an exceptional candidate but also possess unique talents and experiences that will meet their needs. How will you convince them? Which assets will you highlight? What will set your resumé apart from all the others? It is important to identify and understand your differentiators. Use them to draw positive attention to yourself, differentiate yourself from others, and gain the valuable recognition you'll need to be hired and succeed in the company or job of your choice.

In the previous chapter, your assignment was to identify your assets and liabilities. It is now time to reflect on your list of assets. The proper use and promotion of these assets can help set you apart and help bring you recognition for your value and contributions. Proper use of assets includes acting with confidence, not arrogance, and a commitment to pursuing high standards. With such action and attitude, you will be positively recognized. The goal now, is to determine your key differentiators from your list of assets. It is the promotion and highlighting of your key differentiators that will assist you in receiving favorable recognition.

Let's check back with Cheryl (aspires to be a clothing buyer) and Mackenzie (aspires to be vice president of marketing). Both experience difficulties with the concept of product differentiators and how to identify their distinctive assets. They are able to list their assets, but they want to know how they are truly different from the rest of their co-workers and colleagues. How can they develop the confidence that their assets truly are or could become key differentiators? To help them understand this concept, I give them another assignment.

I ask each of them to brainstorm a list of three to five people they admire. Once they list these names, I ask them to think about and write the one quality that, in their minds, made that individual stand out. I am asking them to identify the key differentiator (asset) of that individual and why they believe that asset makes them stand out from the rest of their co-workers and colleagues. To confirm their perceptions, both Cheryl and Mackenzie discuss their comments with each individual. The following lists are the results of this exercise for Cheryl and Mackenzie.

Cheryl's List of Admired People:

NAME	KEY ASSET / DIFFERENTIATOR
Francine (her boss)	Her incredible self-confidence in being the leader of her team – this allows her team to accomplish more projects than they thought possible.
John (a buyer in the men's suits department)	His uncompromising commitment to the customers – has gained him an incredible number of loyal customers and helped increase store revenue.
Sally (an accountant in the finance department)	Her dedication to performing her job without errors – has gained her respect from all those with whom she works.

Mackenzie's List of Admired People:

NAME	KEY ASSET / DIFFERENTIATOR
Linda (the manager of another department)	Her exceptional organizational abilities – this allows her to complete more work than her co-workers because of her time management skills.
George (her boss)	His vast network of contacts – this allows him to take advantage of market trends faster, which results in additional revenue.
Tom (a co-worker; associate marketing manager)	His ability to execute, on-time, all of his objectives – this ability has gained Tom the trust of senior management who knows that no matter what the project, he will complete it on-time and under budget.
Mark (a sales rep)	His extremely professional appearance – this has given him and the company he represents credibility.
Carol (a distributor's rep)	Her outstanding presentation skills – this has earned Carol trust and respect from customers; they trust she knows what she is doing and is looking out for their best interests.

What Cheryl and Mackenzie have found in completing this exercise is that thinking about and identifying each key differentiator was easy because of the confident way in which the individual used that asset and the positive benefits it provided to their jobs.

Further, in talking with these individuals, Cheryl and Mackenzie discover that each has a commitment to high standards – a commitment to be the best they can be in the job they are doing. They back up that commitment with hard work, preparation and the ability to implement their ideas and projects. They also discover that these individuals recognize their own strengths and have used them to further their careers.

For instance, Carol tells Mackenzie that she spent three to four hours preparing the materials for the buyer's presentation a week earlier, adding that she generally spends the same amount of time for all of her important presentations. She says she does this because she realizes the preparation and hard work pay off. Her customers respect her dedication, commitment, expertise, and give her their trust and business in return.

Cheryl speaks with her boss and asks her more about her leadership abilities. Francine remarks, "Sure, hard work is important. But, I made a commitment to myself years ago to be the best manager I can be. I start each day by reminding myself of the positive leader and role model I want to be for my team. This helps me focus my efforts throughout the day so I can prioritize my work around what matters most. It's the old 'first things first' concept." What both Cheryl and Mackenzie realize from this exercise is that the people they admire and who seem unique to them are those who recognize their key differentiators and use them to excel in their careers.

Another lesson learned from the exercise may be discovering what you would like to have as strengths for yourself. It is often human nature to admire people who have qualities we'd like for ourselves. This exercise is a great way to think about the kind of person you'd like to grow to be.

Now it's your turn to complete the same assignment. I want you to quickly brainstorm a list of three to five people you admire. You may know them from work or through another association, such as through volunteer community service work, your church, or school activities, such as a parent/teach association. Write their names on the following table. Then, write down the one differentiator (asset) that immediately comes to mind or stands out about that person and why that differentiator is helpful or beneficial.

Observing the key differentiators of other people will help illustrate how we each possess different and unique strengths and how those strengths can set us apart. It should also help you recognize and appreciate the key strengths you possess. Don't spend too much time on this exercise – just brainstorm it. This exercise should take you no more than 30 minutes.

_____*'s List of Admired People:*

NAME	KEY ASSET / DIFFERENTIATOR

Now that Cheryl and Mackenzie understand the key differentiator of the people they admire, they take on the challenge of determining their own differentiators. They start with their original lists of assets. After reviewing their lists, they identify and prioritize those assets. Cheryl and Mackenzie then write down why they believe each asset is a differentiator. Finally, each of them circles what they believe are their top three assets. Here are their lists:

Cheryl's List of Assets:

ORIGINAL LIST	PRIORITIZED LIST	DIFFERENTIATOR
Organized	1. Organized	People see me as thorough in all my projects and work.
Hard worker	2. Accountable	I am responsible and dependable.
Supportive	3. Hard worker	Others recognize my consistency in execution of projects.
Accountable	4. Supportive	I am a good team member/player; I am helpful.
Professional appearance	5. Professional appearance	The way I look reflects the pride I take in my work.
Good listener	6. Good listener	I respect the opinions and views of others. I care about what they have to say.
Positive attitude	7. Positive attitude	My positive attitude is contagious.

Mackenzie's List of Assets:

ORIGINAL LIST	PRIORITIZED LIST	DIFFERENTIATOR
Creative	1. Creative	People look to me for leading edge ideas.
Expressive	2. Goal oriented	I have a clear idea about what I want to do and how to do it. I am motivated and driven.
Goal oriented	3. Expressive	I communicate with passion because I love what I do.
Decisive	4. Risk taker	I'm not afraid to fail; I'm more willing than others to try new things in order to succeed.
Confident	5. Confident	I believe in myself and believe that I will be successful in my career.
Risk taker	6. Decisive	I'm not afraid to make decisions, even if my decisions are not popular with everyone else.

After working through this exercise, Cheryl and Mackenzie realize they do have assets others recognize and appreciate. Co-workers and managers at the clothing store have come to depend on Cheryl for her ability to complete projects quickly and with high quality. Mackenzie realizes her proven ability to generate fresh ideas and her sense of direction motivates others to seek out her opinion and follow her lead. They can now use these differentiators to draw positive attention to themselves while working on improving their liabilities.

It's time for you to work through the same process as Cheryl and Mackenzie.

- Look back to Chapter 1 where you listed your Assets and Liabilities.
- Write down your original list of assets on the attached template.
- Prioritize your assets with your most distinctive strengths listed on top.
- Write why each asset is or could be a differentiator in the far right column.
- Once you've completed this, draw a circle around your top three assets – these are your key differentiators!

_____'s List of Assets:

ORIGINAL LIST	PRIORITIZED LIST	DIFFERENTIATOR
	1.	
	2.	
	3.	
	4.	
	5.	
	6.	
	7.	
	8.	
	9.	
	10.	

Reminder: Draw a circle around your top three assets.

Great job! Now, keep this list handy, as you'll be coming back to these differentiators later in the book and using them as you work to create your very own personal strategic plan.

"To feel valued, to know, even if only once in a while, that you can do a job well is an absolutely marvelous feeling."
– Barbara Walters

CHAPTER 2:

Strategic Essential

Determine your Differentiators: : *Just as products have strengths that set them apart, so do people. A differentiator is a competitive advantage. Identify those things that you do better than other people. Your distinctive strengths are what others perceive your value to be.*

CHAPTER 3:
Obtain Customer Feedback

"A moment's insight is sometimes worth a life's experience."
— Oliver Wendell Holmes, Sr.

Companies spend millions of dollars each year in market research efforts to discover customer perceptions about their products and services. They conduct this research so they can improve and adapt their products and services in order to sell more. The more a company knows and understands about their customers' perceptions, the more confidence the company has when creating, adapting and marketing their products and services. And, if changes are required later in the process, they are in a better position to know where and how to focus time and resources to make the right changes or enhancements.

Perception is reality. It's as true with people as it is with products. It's understanding how others perceive you that we will explore and test in this chapter. You will learn if your opinion of yourself matches the perception others have of you. In the previous chapters, you identified what you believe to be your assets, liabilities and key differentiators. Now, you need to test those beliefs by seeking the opinions and input of others with whom you work or interact. The goal of this chapter is to assure yourself that you have a realistic understanding of your assets, liabilities and key differentiators.

Cheryl and Mackenzie are asked to choose a minimum of three people with whom they work to be involved in their next exercise. Their assignment is to sit down with each person and obtain his or her comments to the following questions:

- What do you see as my key business assets (strengths)? How would you prioritize these from highest to lowest?
- What do you see as my areas of opportunity for improvement?

Then, based on this feedback, I asked both Cheryl and Mackenzie to re-visit their prioritized list of assets, liabilities and differentiators and explore the following questions themselves:

- Does the information you just received reinforce your opinion or change your opinion of yourself?
- Do you need to make any changes to your list?

Cheryl chose the following people: Francine, her boss; Debra, her co-worker; and Michael, head of accounting. Mackenzie chose the following people: Linda, the manager of another department; Tom, a co-worker; and Alicia, her best friend, an employee at the same company, but in a different department. The feedback Cheryl and Mackenzie received follows:

Cheryl's Feedback:

	FRANCINE (BOSS)	DEBRA (CO-WORKER)	MICHAEL (HEAD OF ACCOUNTING)
KEY ASSETS (PRIORITIZED)	1. Organized 2. Supportive 3. Hard Worker	1. Hard Worker 2. Nice 3. Professional	1. Dependable 2. Organized 3. Accurate
OPPORTUNITIES FOR IMPROVEMENT	• Have more confidence in your capabilities • Be more proactive in taking the lead on projects	• Be more outspoken during department meetings • Show more initiative in taking on new tasks	• Set higher goals

Mackenzie's Feedback:

	LINDA (ANOTHER DEPT. MANAGER)	TOM (CO-WORKER)	ALICIA (BEST FRIEND/ WORKS AT SAME COMPANY)
KEY ASSETS (PRIORITIZED)	1. Creative 2. Willing to lead others 3. Ambitious	1. Energetic 2. Fun to work with 3. Outgoing	1. Confident 2. Risk-taker 3. Creative
OPPORTUNITIES FOR IMPROVEMENT	• Needs to be more focused on assignments; unreliable • Doesn't always "dress for success" • Doesn't always complete projects on time	• Tends to be overly opinionated and critical of others • Doesn't always listen carefully to what people are saying • Not dependable on project teams	• Needs to get over her fear of public speaking

Let's begin with Cheryl. With dinner over, Cheryl makes a cup of tea and sits down to review her feedback and compare it to the list she made of her assets and liabilities. As she reviews the feedback, she smiles. Those who work with her seem to appreciate her and see her assets as she does. That is encouraging. She then reviews the comments on areas for improvement:

- **Have more confidence in your capabilities:** Cheryl thinks about this comment. While she believes she is confident in her skills and abilities, she considers Francine's perception of her and realizes that she may not come across as confident as she feels.

- **Be more proactive in taking the lead on projects:** Cheryl thinks about her last few assignments and concludes that she generally waits for her boss to assign her to a project. She realizes she's never gone to her boss to let her know she would like the opportunity to lead a challenging project. In fact, reflecting on her behavior, she realizes she generally stays within her comfort zone, that is, as a member but never the leader of projects. Cheryl realizes it's time to initiate a change in her relationship with her boss and overcome her reluctance to assume a leadership role.

- **Be more outspoken during department meetings:** Cheryl thinks back on the last few department meetings. She remembers them well. She remembers several people in the department who like to hear themselves talk, oblivious to the fact that they say little of importance. Viewing these soliloquies as a tremendous waste of time that could be better spent actually working on department issues, she often chooses to remain silent. Knowing now that others value her opinions and contributions, she plans to speak out more.
- **Set higher goals:** Cheryl values Michael's input the most. Because of her commitment to her family and her support of their needs, she realizes she hasn't taken the time to establish goals that focus on her career aspirations. Knowing there will always be family obligations, Cheryl, nevertheless, realizes that now is the time to focus on herself. Now is the time to identify the personal growth and satisfaction she wants from her career and the level of commitment she is willing to make to achieve those goals.

After reviewing all of the input, Cheryl concludes that she agrees with the feedback she has received and does not need to update her list. She enjoys feeling appreciated and, after making brownies for her youngest son's school fundraiser, goes to bed with a smile on her face, feeling energized about her future.

Cheryl's Updated Assets and Liabilities List:

ASSETS	LIABILITIES
<ul><li>Organized</li><li>Accountable</li><li>Hard worker</li><li>Supportive</li><li>Professional appearance</li></ul>	<ul><li>Lacks some confidence in certain situations</li><li>Not outspoken</li><li>Need more experience in a leadership role</li></ul>

Mackenzie schedules time to meet with people over a two-day period to obtain their feedback. Back in her office, she re-reads her notes. Her reaction to the feedback is disbelief and anger. "How could so many people make so many negative comments?" she fumes. Instead of receiving the praise she had hoped for, she feels like she was buried by an avalanche of criticism. "It's one thing for me to be down on myself, but it's a different feeling to hear it directly from others." Upset with the unexpected outcome, she grabs her workout bag and heads to the gym.

After taking out her anger in the weight room, Mackenzie returns to her desk. Aware that she was the one who asked for their opinions, and determined to confront this new reality, she focuses on the feedback for improvement. She re-reads the feedback she received:

- **Needs to be more focused on assignments; unreliable:** Mackenzie fully acknowledges that she loves to work on projects. So much so that she has a tendency to take on too many projects, leaving her scrambling to complete them. Mackenzie is aware of this liability, having listed it on an earlier exercise. Until someone else pointed it out, however, she didn't realize the impact it was having on the perception others have of her. While she feels proud of the many projects she had started, she now realizes that others are being affected by what she fails to complete.

- **Doesn't always "dress for success":** Mackenzie looks down at her clothes and laughs, glad that no one else is there at work to see her sitting behind her desk in her workout clothes and baseball hat. She thinks about what she had been wearing earlier that day at work. She has nicer clothes in her closet, but had chosen her clothes that day because she was on deadline with two projects and clothes were the least of her worries. Mackenzie now realizes the importance of dressing for success. Regardless if she has the intelligence, motivation, experience and skills for a job, if she doesn't dress the part, she will make it incredibly difficult to succeed in attaining her aspiration of becoming the vice president of marketing. Mackenzie makes a note to herself that dressing more professionally at work would be in her best interest.

- **Doesn't always complete projects on time / Not dependable on project teams:** Mackenzie realizes that the source of this criticism is the same: she is viewed as unreliable. She willingly takes on too many projects without regard to the commitments she has already made. This results in her becoming overwhelmed and unable to meet her original deadlines. She knows she must become more selective in the assignments she takes on and now realizes the importance of completing them on time.

- **Tends to be overly opinionated and critical of others / Doesn't always listen to what people are saying:** This one really hurts Mackenzie. She thought it was one of her assets to be able to speak up and critique other people and projects. After all, she is merely being expressive! She rationalizes that she never speaks up to hurt people; she speaks up in order to help others improve. Now she hears from Tom, whom she admires, that he views her behavior in this regard as negative and detrimental to the rest of the team. In addition he tells her she has a tendency to form opinions of others too quickly, without listening. Once she forms an opinion, she tunes people out and moves on to other activities – in the middle of department meetings. Mackenzie knows she will have to work hard to repair the damage and change the perception she has created. However, she is motivated by knowing that deep down, she can change her behavior and earn the respect she desires and the respect she needs in order to excel in the company.

- **Needs to get over her fear of public speaking:** Mackenzie already knows she dislikes speaking before large groups. She makes a note to go see her human resources representative to research some classes or seminars on how to become a better public speaker.

In reviewing the feedback, Mackenzie is able to gain new insight. She realizes her perception of herself doesn't fully match the perception of those around her. Now, armed with this information, Mackenzie is in a position to make the changes necessary to improve herself and the perceptions others have of her.

Mackenzie no longer feels angry. She instead feels energized because she now knows the areas she wants to improve. She chooses not to be hurt by the comments but to see them as opportunities for improvement. Mackenzie is determined to make herself into the best and most dazzling product she can be.

Mackenzie's Updated Assets and Liabilities List:

ASSETS	LIABILITIES
• Creative	• Uncomfortable speaking before large groups
• Goal oriented	• Could be more organized
	• Tends to take on too many projects / unreliable
• Expressive	• Poor listener
• Risk-taker	• Sometimes too casual in appearance
• Confident	• Procrastinates
• Decisive	• Judgmental of others / doesn't always listen to what others are saying

Cheryl and Mackenzie have each taken an important step. They have taken the time and made the effort to obtain additional information about themselves from others in order to improve. They are now in a much better position to focus time and resources to make those changes. They are also confident, not only in how they feel about themselves, but confident that their perception of their assets, liabilities and key differentiators align with the perception of those around them.

To thank those people who provided input, Cheryl schedules lunch with each person. Mackenzie decides to send a handwritten thank you note to everyone with whom she spoke.

Just like Cheryl and Mackenzie, you now need to choose at least three people. Your assignment is to sit down with each person and obtain his or her comments to the following questions:

- What do you see as my key business assets (strengths)? How do you see my key strengths as a differentiator? Specifically, how do they distinguish me from other co-workers? In what ways are they truly beneficial to our business? How would you prioritize my strengths from highest to lowest?
- What do you see as my areas of opportunity for improvement?

Here are some helpful hints as you complete this assignment:

- Begin by choosing people whose opinion you value.
- Speak with each person and explain what you are doing. Ask if they would be willing to meet with you to provide feedback. Not everyone will be comfortable providing this kind of feedback – it is important you respect their decision whether or not to participate.
- Schedule a mutually acceptable time and location for the discussion. Be sure to choose a place where both of you are comfortable.
- Be prepared to ask the given questions and any follow up questions to ensure you fully understand their comments.
- Don't be defensive! Just listen to their comments and ask questions to clarify their answers. This is not the time to justify your past behavior. This is an exploratory mission – one where you choose not to take things personally or become offended.
- Use this as an opportunity for discovery, an opportunity to duplicate what companies all over the world do when they research customer perceptions and satisfaction. You are taking an essential step into the business world; you are researching what customers think of your product – **YOU**.
- This can be a very powerful exercise. For some of you, it may confirm the perceptions you already have. Others will find it to be an eye-opening experience. For the most part, you will find that people feel flattered to be a part of your personal development. You may even find that people appreciate your proactive approach toward achieving your goals and aspirations.
- Use this exercise to make a positive impression on those with whom you will be speaking. This is also known as personal marketing.
- Use the following table to capture the feedback. Make some photocopies of the page before you begin, or download the templates from the website.

Feedback From: _____

ASSETS	IMPROVEMENT OPPORTUNITIES

Feedback From: _____

ASSETS	IMPROVEMENT OPPORTUNITIES

Feedback From: _____

ASSETS	IMPROVEMENT OPPORTUNITIES

Based on this feedback, re-visit your original list of assets, liabilities and differentiators. Ask yourself the same questions Cheryl and Mackenzie asked:

- Does the information you just received reinforce your opinion or change your opinion of yourself?
- Do you need to make any changes to your list? Use this opportunity to update your Assets, Liabilities and Differentiators list.

Whenever women complete this exercise, there are always a variety of reactions. Some are similar to Cheryl's reactions and some are very similar to Mackenzie's reactions. Regardless, women find it to be a very enlightening experience. Speaking with others when you are the topic of discussion can be pretty scary, but what I'm sure most of you will find is that the people with whom you speak will be incredibly impressed by your initiative to improve yourself – and you will build respect and admiration from them.

As I stated earlier in this book, in life, perception is often reality. It's important for you to affirm or challenge your own perceptions by seeking input from others, especially those with whom you work and interact on a regular basis. If a discrepancy exists, you need to determine whether to accept the input and make adjustments based on this feedback, or reject the input and work to change the perception of that person. Doing nothing should not be an option.

Stop and consider: How might others perceive you as a product? What people perceive, they believe to be true. If you take on multiple projects but complete none of them, will your co-workers want you on their next project team? If you dress more casually than the company culture, how might others perceive you? Are you being helped or harmed by others' perception of you?

Here is an excellent example of how perception can hurt your career: One day while working for a very large and conservative medical equipment and services company, I walked into the break room to buy a snack. As I walked up to the vending machine I overheard the conversation of a group of women in their early to mid-twenties. One woman commented, "I just can't believe no one around here seems to take me seriously. I'm obviously the best person for the job; I'm the fastest, most skilled and most knowledgeable of everyone who applied. I can't believe I didn't get the position!"

As I turned around to walk out of the break room, I glanced over at the woman who had made the comments. She was wearing a pair of low-waisted jeans, her hair was a mess, there was a ring through her left eyebrow, and a large tattoo was visible on her lower back when she reached across the table for a napkin. This might seem like an extreme example, but if you were the hiring manager at a large, conservative company, how might your perception be affected by this woman's appearance? If the position required interaction with external customers that included hospital administrators and physicians, would her appearance choices help her to market herself above that of her competition?

Remember, *you* know yourself best – you just need to do some calibration to confirm that you are on solid ground and that your own perceptions align with those of the people who know you well.

It's also important that you take feedback from others with a grain of salt. Eleanor Roosevelt once stated, "No one can make you feel inferior without your consent." I've carried this quote with me since the first time I read it and whenever and I'm feeling down, I try to remember those powerful words. So often I see women who allow themselves to be negatively influenced by comments from others who do not have their best interests at heart. Do as I do and try to remember those important words from Eleanor Roosevelt.

*"You've got to take the initiative and play your game...
confidence makes the difference."*
– Chris Evert

CHAPTER 3:

Strategic Essential

Obtain Customer Feedback: *Perception is reality. Seek to understand the perception others have of you. With this knowledge you can be confident of your assessment of your assets, liabilities and differentiators. If you find that a change needs to be made, you are then in a better position to focus your time and efforts to make this happen.*

CHAPTER 4:
Identify and Evaluate your Competitors

"A horse never runs so fast as when he has other horses to catch up and outpace."

— Publius Ovidius Naso

Simply meeting the requirements of the job you seek or the advancement you think you deserve does not mean the job will be given to you. You must compete for that job or that advancement. Competition is a fact of life for most job positions. You must anticipate and prepare for competition.

In today's business environment, even though you might find yourself competing to keep your existing job from being eliminated or outsourced, competition should still be viewed as a positive rather than a negative aspect of your career. Competition can create the need to establish a higher standard of excellence for yourself and can motivate you to improve. Competition can also inspire you to achieve things you never before thought possible, enhancing your sense of accomplishment.

To be the best you can be and to be a viable competitor in the marketplace, you need to understand the internal and external environment in which you are competing. It's not just about understanding the requirements for achieving your aspirations, it's also recognizing there are others competing for that same opportunity – an opportunity often available only to one.

You need to identify and evaluate your competitors to determine if you are fully capable of meeting the requirements for the opportunity you are seeking. This will help you better understand the quality of the individuals with whom you're competing, help you determine your advantages and shortcomings, and help you determine what actions you need to take in order to become more competitive.

Personally, I've come to love competition because it's a way for me to improve myself. When I was a sophomore in high school I had a gymnastics coach who had a tendency to partner me up with the best gymnast on the team (who happened to be three years older than me). At first it really frustrated me because the other gymnast was so much better and I just couldn't keep up with her. When I explained my frustration to the coach she smiled a secretive smile and said, "Exactly! I partnered you with her because she's the best – and you have the potential to become the best too. The only way you're going to get there is if you learn from her and are challenged by her." What a smart woman my coach was!

> *"Compete. Don't envy."*
> – Arabian Proverb

An effective process businesses use to formulate their strategies and to help them assess themselves and their competitors is a S.W.O.T. analysis. S.W.O.T. stands for **Strengths, Weaknesses, Opportunities** and **Threats**. This process captures information about internal strengths and weaknesses as well as external opportunities and threats. Once companies have gathered this S.W.O.T. analysis information, they use it to improve their products and services to better compete in the marketplace.

Creating a S.W.O.T. analysis for yourself is another important step in developing your personal strategic plan. The S.W.O.T. analysis will help you look at your strengths (assets) and weaknesses (liabilities) as well as help you determine the knowledge, capabilities and skills that are necessary to achieve your aspirations. Understanding your weaknesses gives you the ability to determine actions you can take to improve yourself and achieve your desired outcome. Your weaknesses and the strengths of your competitors ultimately become your threats. Your opportunities become the actions and initiatives you can take to overcome your threats and differentiate yourself.

You've already determined your assets, liabilities and differentiators. You have compared your perceptions to the perceptions of your co-workers to bring the two into alignment, if necessary. Now it is time to objectively evaluate your competition.

This next exercise will assist you in better understanding your competition, analyzing job requirements and determining the skills and abilities you need to move past your competitors and achieve your goals and aspirations. After completing your S.W.O.T. analysis, you will list the skills or experiences you need for being in the best position for moving ahead in your career. You will prepare yourself to compete successfully by understanding your current gaps and identifying the specific actions you can take for self-improvement.

Cheryl and Mackenzie will guide you through the exercise. Let's begin with Cheryl. Cheryl's aspiration is to become a clothing buyer. She is aware that there will be an opening for an assistant buyer in the children's clothing department within the next year. It is to Cheryl's advantage that her company's policy is to promote qualified candidates from within the company. For Cheryl, this policy greatly reduces the number of her competitors because it limits applicants to those people already working there. Cheryl's competitors will be those people already working at that company who aspire to obtain the assistant buyer position.

Based on comments in the cafeteria and during various meetings, Cheryl has an idea as to who will be applying for the assistant buyer position. She narrows her list down to the three other candidates she believes are most eligible and interested in applying for the position. Cheryl contacts human resources to obtain a copy of the job description for an assistant buyer. The job description identifies the key requirements and skills necessary for the position. Based on her research, she determines the position will have the following job requirements:

Education and Experience

- Bachelor's Degree in Business / Communications or equivalent work experience.
- Comprehensive understanding of retail environment.
- Knowledge and experience in managing a budget.

Knowledge, Skills and Abilities

- Excellent interpersonal and communication skills.
- Ability to work against deadlines in a fast-paced environment.
- Strong results orientation. Ability to meet and exceed goals consistently.
- Demonstrated success in working individually with minimal supervision.

With this information, Cheryl compares herself and her three competitors against the list of job requirements. She creates a simple chart, listing the job requirements down the left side and her competition across the top. Then, working through each requirement, Cheryl asks herself how she would, as objectively as possible, judge each person's experience/capabilities against the requirement.

Cheryl's completed Competitive Analysis:

REQUIREMENTS	CHERYL	MARY	SUE	JOHN
Current Position	Admin. Asst. to Head Clothing Buyer	Cashier in Cosmetics Department	Admin. Asst. in Finance Department	Sales Associate in Men's Clothing
Bachelor's Degree in Business / Communications or work experience	No degree, 10 years experience	Associate Degree, 4 years experience	No degree, 2 years experience	Bachelor's Degree, 5 years experience
Comprehensive understanding of retail environment	Yes	Yes	Yes	Yes
Knowledge and experience in managing to an assigned budget	No	No	Yes	No
Excellent interpersonal and communication skills	Yes	Yes	No	Yes
Ability to work against deadlines in a fast-paced environment	Yes	Yes	No	Yes
Strong results orientation. Ability to consistently meet and exceed goals	Yes	Not really	No	Yes
Demonstrated success in working individually and under minimal supervision	Yes	No	Yes	Yes
Key Strengths	Work experience, retail knowledge	Fast worker, exceptional customer service skills	Experience with budgets in former job	College degree & years of work experience
Key Weaknesses	Lack of college degree	Not dependable – frequently misses work	Lack of college degree, little work experience	May not have experience with budgets

Based on the above analysis, Cheryl determines her threats (her competitor's strengths) and then determines one initiative (opportunity) she can take to address each of her gaps:

- **Threat #1:** Others in the company have earned their Bachelor's Degrees. Of the potential candidates, Cheryl holds the highest work experience but does not have a college degree. She has determined that at this point in her life, she does not want to go back to school for a degree.

  Opportunity: Cheryl is open to taking classes or seminars to improve specific skills and capabilities. She will identify classes or courses she can take for on-going education and training.

- **Threat #2:** Others in the company have financial business experience. Cheryl lacks experience in managing a budget. Her only experience has been in assisting her manager with her manager's budget.

  Opportunity: Research on the Internet turns up seminars being held in her city on "Finance for the Non-Financial Manager." She intends to sign up for at least the first seminar, hoping that attending will help her better meet this requirement.

- **Threat #3:** Others in the company are more assertive. Cheryl is perceived as being too quiet and as lacking initiative. While Cheryl marked yes in the category excellent interpersonal and communication skills, she realizes that, based on her customer feedback, she has been perceived in the past as being quiet during meetings and lacking initiative in taking on new tasks. Cheryl is determined not to let this perception get in the way of her obtaining this job.

  Opportunity: She resolves to initiate a meeting with the hiring manager to introduce herself and to let the hiring manager know of her goal of applying for and winning the position. This will show the hiring manager that she is serious about being selected for the position. Cheryl will also take the time to ask her existing manager to support her efforts in securing this promotion.

Cheryl's completed S.W.O.T. Analysis:

STRENGTHS (ASSETS)	WEAKNESSES (LIABILITIES)
• Work experience (10 years) • Retail Knowledge	• No college degree • Lack of knowledge and experience managing a budget • Low confidence level in proactively leading projects

THREATS (COMPETITOR STRENGTHS)	OPPORTUNITIES (INITIATIVES)
• Others have Bachelor's Degrees • Others have experience with budgets • Others are more proactive and assertive • John has a degree and strengths in almost all the position requirements	• On-going education through classes and seminars • Sign up for and complete seminar on "Finance for the Non-Financial Manager" • Proactively meet with hiring manager • Proactively meet with boss to secure support and demonstrate my desire to take on this new role • Complete the opportunities listed above and demonstrate that through my 10 years of working, I have gained on-the-job experience equivalent to or exceeding that of a college degree

Cheryl has invested a considerable amount of time in completing this assignment. She is beginning to proactively plan her strategies for achieving her career aspirations.

Mackenzie's aspiration is to become the vice president of marketing in her company or in a similar company in her industry. She realizes she may be competing against others who are potentially working elsewhere in the world. This will make it difficult to evaluate and compare herself with unknown individuals.

Mackenzie determines that her first task will be to survey the job requirements of companies posting open positions for a vice president of marketing. By doing this, she will identify the current market requirements and expectations for the position she desires. She also respects the current vice president of marketing in her company, Brian, and will use him as a standard against which to compare herself.

Mackenzie spends time over several weekends conducting Internet research and summarizing the job requirements she finds posted at various companies' websites. Her compiled list of requirements reads as follows:

- MBA degree
- Minimum 10 years business experience
- Demonstrated success in developing and implementing strategic and tactical marketing and communications plans and programs
- Strong results orientation. Ability to meet and exceed goals consistently. Capable of making commitments, setting priorities, and delivering results on time and on budget
- Broad communication skills and experience involving worldwide interaction and international business
- Demonstrated success in establishing, coordinating and evolving key marketing processes and managing projects to completion
- Excellent organization and presentation skills
- Demonstrated leadership skills to motivate, develop and manage personnel

Keeping in mind this list of requirements, Mackenzie begins to observe Brian doing his job and concludes that he meets all of the requirements and more. Brian has attributes that, in her opinion, make him stand out in the company. She finds him remarkably well organized and competent in managing activities and projects for the marketing department. Brian prioritizes projects and keeps his team on track to complete work on time and under budget. More than any other senior manager in the company, Brian is a leader who motivates his team to achieve more than they ever thought possible. Brian's expertise in managing projects and motivating teams is, without question, the standard to achieving success.

Another idea to help you learn more about someone and what it takes to be competent in a certain job is to ask them for an informational interview. This is where you ask if the person would be willing to sit down with you and discuss their job, job requirements and basically, help you understand the challenges and skills needed for that job. So far, I've never seen anyone turn down a request for an informational interview. Quite the contrary, they've all been excited and very impressed when they've been asked.

Mackenzie's completed Competitive Analysis:

REQUIREMENTS	MACKENZIE	BRIAN
Current Position	Associate Marketing Manager	VP Marketing
MBA Degree	No, only Bachelor's Degree	Yes
10 years business experience	No, 6 years	Yes, 15
Demonstrated success in developing and implementing strategic and tactical marketing and communications plans and programs	Yes	Yes
Strong results orientation; Ability to consistently meet and exceed goals; Capable of making commitments, setting priorities, and delivering results on time and on budget.	No	Yes
Broad communication skills and experience involving worldwide interaction and international business	No	Yes
Demonstrated success in establishing, coordinating and evolving key marketing processes and managing projects to completion	No	Yes
Excellent organization and presentation skills	No	Yes
Demonstrated leadership skills to motivate, develop and manage personnel	No	Yes
Key Strengths	Confident, creative, experience in strategic planning, energetic	Highly organized, great motivator, 3 years experience in VP position
Key Weaknesses	Public speaking, has no experience managing personnel, doesn't always complete projects on time, doesn't always dress professionally	Impatient, prone to working long hours

Because Mackenzie's focus during this exercise is her long-term aspiration (becoming a vice president), she has generated a long list of threats (potential competitor strengths). For her opportunities, she will list possible options and ideas to overcome each threat.

- **Threat #1:** Others have MBA degrees.
  Opportunity: Mackenzie will research MBA programs at colleges and universities in her area. She will determine the cost and time to complete. She may consider night school.

- **Threat #2:** Others have more business experience.
  Opportunity: Mackenzie will continue to work and advance in the field of marketing. She will identify incremental promotional steps.

- **Threat #3:** Others consistently meet and exceed objectives.
  Opportunity: Mackenzie will take classes on time management and project management.

- **Threat #4:** Others have international business experience.
  Opportunity: Mackenzie will seek out participation on future projects in other countries.

- **Threat #5:** Others complete projects on time. Mackenzie realizes she has a tendency to volunteer as a participant on many projects. While she volunteers because she wants to gain experience, she has come to realize she spreads herself too thin. The result is that her projects are not always completed on time.
  Opportunity: Mackenzie will take on fewer projects in order to complete commitments on time.

- **Threat #6:** Others appear to be very comfortable presenting in front of a large audience.
  Opportunity: Mackenzie will take a speech class and will consider taking an acting class. Toastmasters may also be an option.

- **Threat #7:** Others have experience motivating and managing personnel.
  Opportunity: Mackenzie will take classes and read books on effectively managing people. She will seek opportunities which will give her experience managing others.

- **Threat #8:** Others dress more professionally and convey confidence.
  Opportunity: Mackenzie will seek help from an image consultant to provide advice on updating her wardrobe and overall look.

Mackenzie's completed S.W.O.T. Analysis:

STRENGTHS (ASSETS)	WEAKNESSES (LIABILITIES)
• Creative • Goal oriented • Expressive • Risk taker • Confident • Decisive	• No MBA degree • Uncomfortable speaking before large groups • Could be more organized • Tends to take on too many projects / unreliable • Poor listener • Sometimes too casual in appearance • Procrastinates • Judgmental of others / doesn't always listen to what others are saying

THREATS (COMPETITOR STRENGTHS)	OPPORTUNITIES (INITIATIVES)
• Others hold MBA Degrees • Others have extensive business experience • Others consistently meet and exceed objectives • Others have international business experience • Others complete projects on time • Others are comfortable presenting in front of a large audience • Others have experience managing and motivating personnel • Others dress more professionally	• Research MBA programs at colleges and universities in her area. Determine costs and time to complete. Consider night school. • Continue to work and advance in the field of marketing. Identify incremental promotional steps. • Take classes on time and project management. • Seek out participation on future projects that involve geographies outside of the United States. • Take on fewer projects to complete prior commitments on time. • Take a speech class and consider taking an acting class. • Take some classes on effectively managing people. Seek out promotional opportunities that would provide experience in managing others. • Seek help from an image consultant.

Like Cheryl, Mackenzie has invested considerable time and care in organizing the steps she needs to take to realize her goals. Since some of the initiatives will require time and effort to complete, at least she can now focus on what she needs to accomplish. Mackenzie is excited and re-energized. Her mantra each morning has become, "Onward and upward!"

You need to determine if any of your aspirations involve a competitive environment. Try your best to determine your competitors. You may be competing with colleagues you know or can identify. Or, your competitors may be people from other companies or elsewhere in the world. In either case, you need to clearly identify and document the requirements of the position you seek. You will also need to understand the strengths and weaknesses of your competitors. Completing this exercise will ensure that you know how to prepare yourself with the skills and experience that will differentiate you from your competition.

Following are some helpful hints and several templates to guide you through the steps necessary to complete your S.W.O.T analysis:

- The position you select to evaluate may be short-term or long-term. Use this exercise to help you focus your actions toward the most effective way of meeting the requirements and qualifying for consideration for that position.
- To obtain position requirements for your desired position try:
    1) contacting your human resources department;
    2) searching your company's internal website; and
    3) searching the Internet for job bulletin boards showing position requirements.
- You may be searching for position requirements for a job that is not currently posted. Mackenzie, for example, searched for the job description for the vice president of marketing, a position that was currently filled. In general, human resource departments will have job descriptions on file for every job in the company. Just put in a request for the description you need.
- As you complete the template, list as many job specific requirements as you can.
- In identifying your competition, limit your list to those whom you feel have a realistic chance of being selected for the position, not those who have shown a casual interest.
- You may not know your direct competitors for a position. That's okay – don't let this stop you. Like Mackenzie, you can use either known criteria / requirements or an individual currently holding the position to evaluate yourself.
- As you determine threats and opportunities, it is important not only to look at your competitors' strengths, but also to consider your own key weaknesses as well.
- Make some photocopies of the page before you begin, or download the templates from the website. *(See page 105 for more information.)*

Requirements for _____ position:

REQUIREMENTS
1.
2.
3.
4.
5.
6.
7.
8.
9.
10.

_____'s Competitive Analysis:

REQUIREMENTS	YOUR NAME	COMPETITOR	COMPETITOR	COMPETITOR
Current Position				
Key Strengths				
Key Weaknesses				

_____'s S.W.O.T. Analysis:

STRENGTHS (ASSETS)	WEAKNESSES (LIABILITIES)
• _____	• _____
• _____	• _____
• _____	• _____
• _____	• _____
• _____	• _____
• _____	• _____

THREATS (COMPETITOR STRENGTHS)	OPPORTUNITIES (INITIATIVES)
• _____	• _____
• _____	• _____
• _____	• _____
• _____	• _____
• _____	• _____
• _____	• _____

Congratulations! You have completed the exercise. The purpose of the S.W.O.T. analysis is to identify the key actions you will need to take to best meet the requirements of the job; after all, the goal is to prepare yourself to be the best candidate for the position to which you aspire.

After reading this chapter and completing the exercises, the following is a list of key questions to which you should now be able to answer, "Yes":

- Have I identified the requirements of the position that I seek? (Education, experience, skills and abilities, etc.)
- Have I identified my key competitors?
- Do I understand how my qualifications meet the job requirements?
- Do I understand how my qualifications must exceed those of my key competitors?
- Do I understand the gaps between the job requirements and my qualifications?
- Do I understand the gaps between my qualifications and those of my key competitors?
- Have I identified specific actions I can take to compensate for each identified gap?

I personally use these exercises every time I am applying and interviewing for a new position. Going through this process helps ensure I'm prepared for the interview process and gets me ready to answer tough questions from the interviewers. It also helps me better understand the position and the actual work that will be required. And, by following this process, I can anticipate areas that could be potential issues. That way I can either gain the necessary skills and experience prior to applying for the job or pull together my plan of action for learning the skills on the job (in the new position) and discuss my plan with the hiring manager.

Often times, during the interview, I actually explain to the hiring manager the process I've gone through to ensure I'm qualified for the position. The hiring managers have always been impressed with the homework I've done on the position and the thought process I've gone through to make sure that it's a good fit for my skills, abilities and personality type.

Remember, identifying and evaluating the competition helps keep you at your best because it encourages you to continuously improve yourself and your skills. Your goal is to sharpen your *Strengths,* improve your *Weaknesses,* identify *Opportunities* for improvement and neutralize or overcome your *Threats.* Always compete to be the best you can be!

"Competition is easier to accept if you realize that it is not an act of aggression. I've worked with my best friends in direct competition. Whatever you want in life other people are going to want it, too. Believe in yourself enough to accept the idea that you have an equal right to it."

– Diane Sawyer

CHAPTER 4:

Strategic Essential

Identify and Evaluate your Competitors: *Competition is a fact of life. Simply doing your job and hoping for the best is not enough. You need to compete for what you want. Competition and what you can learn from it should be viewed positively and embraced. Strive to be your best by understanding yourself and your competitors.*

CHAPTER 5:
Determine your Goals

"A goal without a plan is just a wish."

— Antoine de Saint-Exupery

Surely, at one time or another we have all felt frustrated because we have failed to accomplish more in the course of our careers. Or, we've looked back on the last year and felt discouraged because we failed to complete some of our New Year's resolutions. Despite starting strong and confident, we failed to achieve what we sought. Simply announcing that we want to improve ourselves rarely results in the outcome for which we had hoped. Merely saying that we want something is different from making the effort to create a well-defined written action plan.

It has been my experience that individuals with clearly written goals are more successful. They enjoy more success because their goals are supported by defined action statements that describe the steps they will take to accomplish their goals.

Goals reflect our aspirations and enable us to achieve them. Our goals, which we must first define, are the short and long term stepping stones we use to incrementally reach our desired destination. By using the goal-setting process, we can turn our liabilities into assets and our weaknesses into strengths.

The quality of the goals we set will determine their effectiveness. One technique to consider using when creating your goals is S.M.A.R.T. *(Specific, Measurable, Attainable, Relevant and Time-bound)*. Countless businesses and successful individuals throughout the world use this technique. While over the years many variations have been created, S.M.A.R.T. continues to embody sound principles for the process of creating goals.

Looking at each component of the S.M.A.R.T. goal setting model will help you better understand the concept and the difference between poorly defined goals and clearly, succinctly written goals.

S = Specific

Goals need to be explicit and detailed. They should be clear and unambiguous. Accomplishing a vague goal is time-consuming and frustrating. Answering the questions of *Who, What, When, Where, How* and *To What Extent* will help assure that your goal is specific.

Example

* Poorly defined goal: I want to be a better speaker.
* Specific goal: Within one year, I want to have completed both a PowerPoint training class and a speech course. I will join Toastmasters within six months.

M = Measurable

Your goal must have a specific outcome against which you can measure your progress and determine completion. You need to establish concrete criteria in defining what specifically will be measured. Goals that cannot be measured are difficult to complete. You will be further motivated when you see the tangible results as you make progress in achieving your goal.

Example

* Poorly defined goal: I want to take a writing class soon.
* Measurable goal: I will complete a writing class at a local community college within the next 12 months and achieve a grade of "B" or higher.

A = Attainable

Goals must allow you to stretch yourself but still be reasonable. Goals which are set too high or which are not achievable will only discourage you. On the flip side, goals set too low will be of very little value. Achieving reasonable goals that truly challenge you will build your confidence to take on greater challenges with each success.

Example

* Poorly defined goal: I would like to be the best at everything I do.
* Attainable goal: I am going to select one business-related topic (e.g. leadership, personnel management, finance, marketing) each year and read one book every three months on that topic so I can achieve additional knowledge in one topic every year.

R = Relevant

Each goal must have meaning for you. Goals need to be adequately resourced and set with a realistic expectation of success. Each goal should be supportive of your aspiration and consistent with your other goals. Remember, you are setting the goal to make progress toward a desired end. Create an emotional attachment to your goal. This will result in your being more passionate about accomplishing it and will help you maintain your commitment.

Example

* Poorly defined goal: I really want to be a vice president of the company.
* Relevant goal: I want to be the Supervisor of the Billing department within the next two years because my skills and interest make me the best choice for this position.

T = Time-Bound

Goals must clearly define a beginning and an ending. Determining a fixed duration provides structure and motivation. The length of time from start date to end date must support the purpose of the goal. Initiatives should be used to manage goals that are long term. An initiative is a project, program, class, book, milestone or something you will do that will allow you to take an incremental step toward achieving your aspiration. Completing initiatives / milestones assist you in maintaining focus by helping you monitor your progress and keep you on track. They are the destinations you must reach on your roadmap in order to achieve your final destination (your aspiration). So, challenge yourself but work within realistic time lines to keep your goals relevant to your overall plan.

Example

* Poorly defined goal: I will work to improve myself in business.
* Time-Bound goal: I will identify one liability and, during the next six months, complete at least one seminar and read at least two books on that subject to improve my expertise in that area.

When setting long-term goals, you may need to identify shorter-term initiatives to use as stepping-stones. Let's use a simple sports analogy from my past experience. A while back I decided to take up running to help me stay healthy and improve my physical fitness. An example of my long-term goal supported by initiatives was to complete a half marathon in less than two hours and fifteen minutes within three months. Accomplishing this goal required achieving several shorter-term initiatives, which included:

- Running a total of at least 25 miles a week for the three months leading up to the half marathon
- Joining a gym within two weeks and beginning cross-training on weights
- Completing a 5k running race in under 30 minutes within 30 days
- Completing a 10k running race in under 60 minutes within 60 days
- Running 12 miles in under two hours within 75 days

By setting shorter-term initiatives and working to accomplish them step-by-step, I was able to complete my long-term goal and ran in a Seattle-area half marathon (and I achieved my time objective!). The great part about breaking down long-term goals into shorter-term initiatives is that it keeps me from feeling overwhelmed. It also keeps me motivated because I see the progress I'm making as I complete the short-term initiatives and check them off my list.

It takes some time and practice, but you will soon be comfortable setting long-term goals. As you determine your long-term goals, make sure you consider the shorter-term steps or initiatives it will take to reach those goals.

Goals and aspirations are not gender specific; so don't let anything stop you from setting and achieving the goals you want to accomplish. I have succeeded at business and in my career in areas that have been traditionally male dominated. I spent many years as the first and only female on the senior service management team for a medical equipment company and I am a much better person in business for having gained that experience. I also helped pave the way for other women to enter this area of business by demonstrating to the men involved that I was not only just as competent, but that I was also able to bring a female approach and perspective to the business. I earned their respect. As Mary Kay Ash, the founder of Mary Kay, Inc. once said, "The truth is that thinking like a woman can be a tremendous advantage."

Being female can actually be to your benefit when breaking into areas of business that have been male dominated. Nina DiSesa, chairman and chief creative officer of McCann-Erickson was once quoted as saying, "…I'm not suggesting that the men in the office need to weep at the movies. I'm simply trying to help us all embrace what we generally think of as female attributes: teamwork, relationship-building, collaboration and empathy. Some people call this 'Emotional Intelligence' and its become the paradigm for effective leadership. Mothers and wives have been doing this since the beginning of time." Thriving in traditionally male dominated businesses requires women who are unafraid to earn the respect of their male colleagues and who are resilient, energetic, and confident enough to always be themselves and never try to imitate the men. So, don't be afraid to set goals or aspirations in areas that have previously been considered the domain of males.

Also, do not be afraid to make lateral career moves. In order to gain the necessary experience to be good at higher-level positions, you must be willing to learn all aspects of business and you must learn how to motivate and manage personnel. This means you need to take the initiative to set goals and seek positions that will provide you with the opportunity to broaden your experience and increase your skills, especially in the areas of business operations and running P&Ls (running departments with responsibility for profit and loss). It is a rare occasion that someone who has experience in only one area of business rises to the highest-level positions in a company. To be good in business you need to understand many aspects, from sales, service, marketing and operations to finance, human resources and legal requirements.

Goal setting is a skill. Don't expect mastery overnight. You will find, however, the more you use the technique the easier it will become to establish the written S.M.A.R.T. goals that will provide you with the confidence you need to take action in your life.

> "The big secret in life is that there is no big secret. Whatever your goal, you can get there if you're willing to work."
> – Oprah Winfrey

It's time to begin the work of defining the goals that will lead to achieving your aspirations. It's time to use this S.M.A.R.T. technique to diminish your liabilities and weaknesses and enhance your assets and strengths. This process involves determining what you need to do and how long it will take to do it. It's time to get organized.

Let's take a look at goal setting through the experiences of Cheryl and Mackenzie. We last left Cheryl excited about getting organized and determining her goals. She reviews her S.W.O.T. analysis and lists her overall goals and initiatives in support of achieving her aspiration to become a clothing buyer. Her completed list follows:

Cheryl's List of Goals:

GOALS	INITIATIVES	TIMING
Increase my understanding of the financial aspects of the clothing business by completing classes and taking on additional agreed upon tasks from my manager to utilize the new skills I will acquire.	• Enroll and complete the seminar on "Finance for the Non-Financial Manager." • Meet with my manager to identify specific new job responsibilities that can be assigned to me to support my developing financial skills and expertise.	Winter Quarter March
Fine-tune my skills and abilities in communications to facilitate my taking on leadership roles and projects.	• Enroll in and complete a Speech class. • Purchase and read 3 books on Communications to improve my understanding of both the types of media and the ways media is used to communicate.	Spring Quarter Spring
Become more adept at leading projects by means of education and on-the-job training to increase my professional visibility and my contribution to the store.	• Enroll in and complete a seminar on using Project Management software so I can effectively track projects, resources and accomplishments. • Work with my manager to identify a project I can lead.	December December

We know that Mackenzie's goals focus on becoming the vice president of marketing, her key aspiration. As a result of completing the previous exercises, Mackenzie has identified a number of liabilities she must overcome in order to achieve this aspiration. Utilizing the S.M.A.R.T. technique, she reviews her liabilities and translates them into actions she can take. Mackenzie's completed list follows:

Mackenzie's List of Goals:

GOALS	INITIATIVES	TIMING
Complete my Masters Degree in Business Administration within the next four years by enrolling in night school.	• Meet with HR, apply for financial assistance and letter of recommendation.	November
	• Register for one class per quarter beginning with the Winter quarter.	December
	• Ensure Project Management is one of the first classes I complete within first year of study.	Within 1 year
Ensure I complete my projects on time and I meet and exceed all commitments to others – beginning immediately.	• Complete a Time Management seminar.	January
	• Begin using time management software and tools.	Immediate
Overcome my fear of speaking in front of large groups by the end of this year.	• Enroll in and complete a Speech class.	Spring Quarter
	• Join and participate in Toastmasters.	Immediate
	• Work with manager to identify an upcoming training session for the Field Team I can lead.	Summer
	• Find an image consultant.	Immediate
Become a Marketing Manager responsible for personnel and budget management within the next 18 months.	• Meet with manager; explain aspiration to become a marketing manager.	Immediate
	• Review initiatives I need to complete to achieve this level of management within the company.	Immediate
	• Meet with HR; determine available internal and external leadership training opportunities.	Fall
	• Work with manager to identify projects with international scope to learn international markets.	Fall

By simply working through this exercise, both Cheryl and Mackenzie feel a new sense of commitment and motivation. They now see the beginning of a plan with the actions necessary to make their dreams a reality. It is empowering to move from merely knowing what you want, to identifying the specific actions you will take. Empower yourself to succeed!

Now, let's take the steps to make *your* dreams and aspirations a reality through continuous improvement. You will complete the same exercise as Cheryl and Mackenzie. Here are some helpful hints as you work through your assignment:

- Begin by reviewing your S.W.O.T. analysis. Prioritize the areas on which to focus to improve your strengths and overcome your weaknesses as you move closer to achieving your aspirations.
- Using the S.M.A.R.T. goal-setting technique, write down specific goals and supporting initiatives.
- You may have similar goals as Cheryl and Mackenzie or you may have completely different goals. Your goals should be relevant to *your* aspirations.
- Remember, you don't necessarily need to take formal classes or seminars to learn new skills or broaden your knowledge. You can borrow books from friends, buy used books, and read books from the public library for very little cost. You can also search the Internet for free seminars. I also recommend you check to see if your workplace sponsors seminars or training programs or if they offer an education reimbursement program. You don't have to be rich, you just have to get a little creative and do some research!
- If you have a goal to learn a new skill, learn about another business or learn another area within a business, one way to gain experience is through volunteer work. Think about creative ways you could volunteer your time and services. For example, you could ask to help out on projects in another department or volunteer in your community. If you are getting back into the workplace after taking time off to raise your children or just starting out looking for a job after finishing school, you can also approach various companies and ask if they would allow you to volunteer some of your time in order to gain experience.

- Many women may not think about networking as a goal. It has been my experience that women tend to spend less time networking than men. However, networking is a great way to get to know people in your community, in your existing workplace and in other businesses. It helps you expand your circle of friends, provides additional contacts for current and future job opportunities and helps create a solid support system as you move forward in your career. *Networking should be a key part of every woman's career.* You can network with other women through local branches of women's networks (check for listings on the Internet), through church groups, book clubs, community groups, your children's Parent Teacher Association (PTA), your workplace, and many other places. A good friend of mine checked with her local Chamber of Commerce and found an existing Women's Executive Network she was able to join. Get creative and chat with other women for networking ideas and opportunities.

- Have fun with this exercise! Visualize coaching yourself to achieve the highest degree of excellence.

- Remember, this is a new skill you will be practicing. You shouldn't expect perfection in clarifying your goals the first time.

- Set aside adequate time to reflect on your most meaningful goals.

- Write an initial draft and then set it aside. Come back to it a day or two later after you've had time to reflect on what you have written.

- Before beginning the exercise, make extra copies of the table or download the templates from the website to record the information. *(See page 105 for more information.)*

- Remember, any dream is a dream worth pursuing. Reach for the stars and achieve your dreams!

As you work through this exercise, here is a list of essential skills I recommend you consider developing. These are obviously skills everyone could develop.

- **Listening and Understanding:** The ability to listen to others in a caring and compassionate way without the intent to reply, in an effort to understand their situation and from where they are coming emotionally.
- **Public Speaking:** The ability to speak publicly before a group of any size.
- **Writing:** The ability to compose concise and easily understood emails, memos and presentations.
- **Time Management:** The ability to analyze and manage efficiency in the workplace – maximizing productivity while remaining accessible to co-workers.
- **Project Management:** The ability to take a project and successfully manage it from inception to completion.
- **Recognizing Work Styles:** The ability to recognize and accommodate different styles of working. People work in different ways: some are fast paced, driven and unemotional; others are outgoing and talkative; some are quiet and enjoy analytical data; still others are personable and non-confrontational. Understand that no work style is superior to others. Be accommodating and flexible in your work style in order to facilitate a productive work environment.
- **Priority Setting:** The ability to prioritize and focus on completing high priority work rather than lower priority activities.

Helpful hints for setting goals:

- Goals should be written utilizing the S.M.A.R.T. technique.
- Goals should be reviewed frequently.
- Goals need to be visualized. You must see it and believe in it to achieve it.
- Goals may require corrective action. Remember that goals provide feedback.
- Goals need to be consistent, not in conflict with one another.
- Goals need to call for action.

_____'s List of Goals:

GOALS	INITIATIVES	TIMING

"Failure to hit the bull's eye is never the fault of the target.
To improve your aim – improve yourself."
– Gilbert Arland

CHAPTER 5:

Strategic Essential

Determine your Goals: *Goals reflect what you want to accomplish to improve yourself. They are your targets, both short-term and long-term. Goal setting will lead you to a greater sense of commitment and motivation as you pursue your aspirations.*

CHAPTER 6:
Create your Strategic Plan

"The distance is nothing; it's only the first step that is difficult."
— Marquise Du Deffand

Like using a roadmap to arrive at a destination, having a clear plan in place will help you achieve your aspirations in the shortest period of time and in the most efficient manner. When you completed the first five chapters of this book, you took the first and most challenging steps toward creating your career, your way. The next step in the process is to develop a strategic plan.

The strategic plan is the roadmap for a company. The strategic plan provides a clear sense of direction, defines goals to be accomplished, identifies those individuals accountable for achieving goals, and determines the timelines and resources required for success. A company's strategic plan also defines how progress will be measured in order to monitor the plan, determine its progress and anticipate the date of completion. In this chapter, we will follow the concept of a business strategic plan, which I have simplified to make it easier to use in the context of career development.

Before you write your strategic plan, you need to make sure you have identified your destination and defined, in writing, your aspiration. Then you will identify the components that support your aspiration, as you begin to create a visual roadmap.

Both Cheryl and Mackenzie have clearly defined their aspirations. We know that Cheryl aspires to become a clothing buyer. Mackenzie aspires to become the vice president of marketing. Each has established goals beyond merely receiving a promotion or moving up. Like Cheryl and Mackenzie, as you approach this next exercise, you will need to be both comfortable and confident in describing your aspiration in a clear, concise manner.

As you determine and clarify your aspiration, consider the following points: First, it is essential to identify what makes you happy and what you find rewarding. Second, this may be a long journey, which will require you to remain focused and disciplined. Third, you will face barriers along the way. Are you willing and able to put in the hours and time necessary to complete a college degree by going to school at night? Are you willing to spend personal time on the weekends reading books to help you improve your knowledge of different subjects? Are your defined aspirations important enough for you to remain committed, even when you confront barriers along the way? If not, continue to clarify your aspirations until you can say, "Yes!"

Working toward and achieving your aspiration is to be commended! Seeking and achieving fulfillment and recognition in your career can motivate and energize you to remain committed to achieving your aspiration. Seeking to be recognized for outstanding work is an essential goal for all working women.

Achieving your aspirations is a continuous process. Once you have achieved an aspiration, others will follow. You will find that achieving your ambitions and remaining committed to yourself will build the confidence and the skills you will need to successfully assume new and even greater challenges.

I created the following template to simplify the information you will need for your personal strategic plan. You have already mastered the skills and techniques as you completed the exercises in chapters one through five. Now your efforts will culminate in your creating a one-page personal strategic plan. Let's take a look at the one-page strategic plan template on the following page, broken down by section with explanations given for each section.

Personal Strategic Plan – Template

ASPIRATION	GOALS	INITIATIVES	TIMING	MEASUREMENT	STATUS
1	6	7	8	9	10
ASSETS					
2					
LIABILITIES					
3					
DIFFERENTIATORS					
4					
THREATS					
5					

Personal Strategic Plan – Template Key

Section 1: Aspiration
- Record your aspiration.

Section 2: Assets – Chapter 1
- State your assets (strengths).

Section 3: Liabilities – Chapter 1
- Prioritize and state your liabilities (weaknesses).

Section 4: Differentiators – Chapter 2
- State your differentiators.

Section 5: Threats – Chapter 4
- State your threats using your S.W.O.T. analysis information.

Section 6: Goals – Chapter 5
- Use your S.M.A.R.T. goals to complete this section.

Section 7: Initiatives – Chapter 5
- Break down your goals into the actionable and measurable milestones (initiatives) you expect to complete.
- Update your one-page strategic plan monthly to reflect items you have completed or to make minor adjustments.

Section 8: Timing – Chapter 5
- Fill in the timing for each initiative you have identified.

Section 9: Measurement – Chapter 5
- Determine and record what will indicate the completion of each initiative.

Section 10: Status – Chapter 8
- Each month, fill in the updated progress you have made on each initiative.

Now that you understand the purpose and layout of the template, let's review the work Cheryl and Mackenzie have done to complete their strategic plans.

Cheryl's Aspiration, Goals, Initiatives and Timing

Goal 1: I will increase my understanding of the financial aspects of business by completing classes and taking on additional agreed upon tasks from my manager to utilize my new skills.

Initiative 1a: Enroll in and complete the seminar "Finance for the Non-Financial Manager."
Timing: Winter (January – March)

Initiative 1b: Meet with my manager to identify specific new job responsibilities I can be assigned which will support my development of financial skills and expertise.
Timing: March

Goal 2: I will expand my skill and ability in communications in order to be in a better position for taking on leadership roles and projects.

Initiative 2a: Enroll in and complete a speech class to improve my presentation skills.
Timing: Spring Quarter (April – June)

Initiative 2b: Read three books on Communications to improve my understanding of the types of media and the ways media is used to communicate.
Timing: Spring

Goal 3: I will become more adept at leading projects by means of education and on-the-job training to increase my professional visibility and my contribution to the store.

Initiative 3a: Enroll in and complete a seminar on using Project Management software so I can effectively track projects, resources and initiatives.
Timing: December

Initiative 3b: Work with my manager to identify a project I can lead.
Timing: December

Mackenzie's Aspiration, Goals, Initiatives and Timing

Goal 1: I will complete my Masters Degree in Business Administration within the next four years by enrolling in night school.

> Initiative 1a: Meet with HR, apply for financial assistance and request a letter of recommendation (check into company policy for tuition reimbursement).
> Timing: November
>
> Initiative 1b: Register for one class per quarter beginning with the Winter Quarter.
> Timing: December
>
> Initiative 1c: Ensure that Project Management is a class I complete within my first year of study.
> Timing: Within one year

Goal 2: I will complete my projects on time and I will meet and exceed all commitments to others – beginning immediately.

> Initiative 2a: Enroll in and complete a time management seminar.
> Timing: January
>
> Initiative 2b: Begin using time management software and tools to manage my commitments daily.
> Timing: Immediate

Goal 3: I will overcome my fear of speaking in front of large groups by taking a speech class; I will improve my image; and I will obtain additional on-the-job experience by the end of this year.

> Initiative 3a: Enroll in and complete a speech class.
> Timing: Spring Quarter (April - June)
>
> Initiative 3b: Join and participate in Toastmasters' activities to gain confidence in public speaking and improve my listening skills.
> Timing: Immediate
>
> Initiative 3c: Work with my manager to identify an opportunity for me to lead the training of our field team on our products and services.
> Timing: Summer
>
> Initiative 3d: Find a personal image consultant to help me improve my overall look to one that is more professional.
> Timing: Immediate

Goal 4: I will become a marketing manager responsible for personnel and budget management within two years.

> Initiative 4a: Meet with my current manager to explain my aspiration to be a marketing manager and brainstorm with her the initiatives I need to complete to achieve this level of management within the company.
> Timing: Immediate

> Initiative 4b: Meet with a human resources representative to determine what internal and external leadership training opportunities are available.
> Timing: Immediate

> Initiative 4c: Work with my manager to identify opportunities to work on projects of a global scope to become more familiar with the markets outside the United States.
> Timing: Fall

Cheryl's and Mackenzie's completed templates summarize the information and skills each of them developed as they worked through the earlier exercises. By recording this information on one page, each can clearly see her personal roadmap to achieving her aspirations. Their personal strategic plans will help Cheryl and Mackenzie work smarter, not just harder, to achieve their career aspirations.

I have seen women with the greatest intentions attempt to achieve their ambitions with no well thought out plan. These are the cases that ultimately either fail to work out or take a very long time to achieve. Save yourself time and headaches by getting organized with a plan!

Before you begin to write your own strategic plan, I recommend you review Cheryl and Mackenzie's completed strategic plans, which are shown on the following pages.

Cheryl's Strategic Plan:

ASPIRATION	GOALS	INITIATIVES	TIMING	MEASUREMENT	STATUS
Become a Clothing Buyer	**Goal 1:** Increase my understanding of financial aspects of business by completing classes and taking on additional agreed upon tasks from my manager to utilize my new skills.	**1a:** Enroll in and complete the seminar "Finance for the Non-Financial Manager."	**1a:** Winter	**1a:** Certificate of completion.	
		1b: Meet with my manager to identify specific new job responsibilities I can be assigned which will support my development of financial skills and expertise.	**1b:** March	**1b:** Mutually agreed upon minutes.	
ASSETS • Organized • Accountable • Hard worker	**Goal 2:** Expand my skills and abilities in communications in order to be in a better position to facilitate taking on leadership roles and projects.	**2a:** Enroll in and complete a speech class to improve my presentation skills.	**2a:** Spring Quarter	**2a:** Certificate of completion. Passing grade, "B" or better.	
LIABILITIES • Lack confidence • Not outspoken • Lack leadership experience		**2b:** Purchase and read 3 books on Communications to improve my understanding of the types of media and the ways media is used to communicate.	**2b:** Spring	**2b:** Certificate of completion. Passing grade, "B" or better.	
DIFFERENTIATORS • Thorough • Responsible and dependable • Consistent in execution of projects • Team player • Professional appearance	**Goal 3:** Become more adept at leading projects by means of education and on-the-job training to increase my professional visibility and my contribution to the store.	**3a:** Enroll in and complete a seminar on using Project Management software so I can effectively track projects, resources and initiatives.	**3a:** December	**3a:** Certificate of completion. Passing grade, "B" or better.	
THREATS • People with college degrees • People with financial experience • People who are proactive and assertive		**3b:** Work with my manager to identify a project I can lead.	**3b:** December	**3b:** Phase 1 – assigned project; Phase 2 – project kick off; Phase 3 – completion of project.	

Mackenzie's Strategic Plan:

ASPIRATION	GOALS	INITIATIVES	TIMING	MEASUREMENT	STATUS
Become the Vice President of Marketing	**Goal 1:** Complete my Masters Degree in Business Administration within the next four years by enrolling in night school.	**1a:** Meet with HR, apply for financial assistance and letter of recommendation.	**1a:** November	**1a:** Written approval and letter.	
		1b: Register for one class per quarter beginning with the Winter quarter.	**1b:** December	**1b:** Complete registration.	
		1c: Ensure that Project Management is one of the first classes I complete within my first year of study.	**1c:** Within one year	**1c:** Certification of completion. Passing grade.	
	Goal 2: Complete my projects on time and meet and exceed all commitments to other.	**2a:** Enroll in and complete a time management seminar.	**2a:** January	**2a:** Certification of completion.	
		2b: Begin using time management software and tools to manage my commitments daily.	**2b:** Immediate	**2b:** Completed calendar.	
	Goal 3: I will overcome my fear of speaking in front of large groups by taking a speech class; I will improve my image; and I will obtain additional on-the-job experience by the end of this year.	**3a:** Complete a speech class.	**3a:** Spring Quarter	**3a:** Certification of completion.	
		3b: Join and participate in Toastmasters' activities.	**3b:** Immediate	**3b:** Attend 3 meetings.	
		3c: Work with manager to identify an opportunity to lead the training of our field team.	**3c:** Summer	**3c:** Complete training session.	
		3d: Find a personal image consultant to help me improve my overall look to one that is more professional.	**3d:** Immediate	**3d:** Receive recommendations.	
	Goal 4: Become a marketing manager responsible for personnel and budget management within the next 18 months.	**4a:** Meet with my current manager to explain my aspiration to be a marketing manager and brainstorm with her the initiatives I need to complete to achieve this level of management within the company.	**4a:** Immediate	**4a:** Agreed upon objectives document.	
		4b: Meet with HR, determine what internal and external leadership training opportunities are available.	**4b:** Immediate	**4b:** Complete identified training.	
		4c: Work with manager to identify opportunities to work on projects of a global scope to become more familiar with the markets outside the U.S.A.	**4c:** Fall	**4c:** Complete one international project.	

ASSETS
- Creative
- Goal Oriented
- Expressive

LIABILITIES
- Fear of public speaking
- Unorganized
- Take on too many projects
- Too casual in attire

DIFFERENTIATORS
- Leading edge ideas
- Motivated and driven
- Communicate with passion
- Not afraid to fail
- Confident

THREATS
- People with MBAs
- People with extensive business experience
- People with international experience
- People with public speaking skills
- People with personnel management experience
- Professionally dressed people

Now it's your turn. Your mission is to create your personal strategic plan. Your work may take several hours. Don't get discouraged. Your time will be well invested (and you are worth the investment!). Here are some helpful hints to follow as you complete this exercise:

- Before you start this exercise make sure you have your updated list of assets and liabilities handy.
- For each component of the strategic plan, keep your comments concise; focus only on your highest priorities.
- Be realistic on the time you allow yourself to complete each initiative. For example, a goal of completing two to three classes and a seminar within one quarter while working full-time is pretty unrealistic. Your roadmap should energize you, not exhaust you!
- Feel free to modify some of your earlier statements or work. Consider this a living document that you will continue to update over time, adding new goals and initiatives as you complete existing ones.
- When you define your measurements, try to identify a tangible event or document (see Cheryl's strategic plan) to denote completion of that initiative.
- If you have not listed all the initiatives needed to complete a goal, that's fine. As initiatives are completed, others will be added. Again, this is a living document you will update as needed.
- Make photocopies of the template before you begin.
- If you prefer to create your strategic plan electronically, just log onto the website at **www.careerwomaninc.com** and click on "**Resources**" – then just look for this book and you may download the templates after you enter the password, "**Athena**".
- Finally, remember, this document does not have to be perfect. You aren't being graded on it.

Have fun with the exercise; I hope you learn a lot about yourself!

_____'s Strategic Plan:

ASPIRATION	GOALS	INITIATIVES	TIMING	MEASUREMENT	STATUS
ASSETS					
LIABILITIES					
DIFFERENTIATORS					
THREATS					

You have come a long way by completing this chapter. You now have something only a fraction of people around the world possess – you have a plan! Hopefully this document reflects who you are and what you wish to achieve. You can now use your strategic plan to control your destiny and your future. Your success will not be an accident or a product of luck. Achieving your aspiration directly depends upon your drive, dedication and focused commitment to executing your strategic plan.

*"If you always do what you've always done
you will always be where you've always been."*
– Anonymous

CHAPTER 6:

Strategic Essential

Create your Strategic Plan: *Like using a roadmap to arrive at a destination, having a clear plan in place helps assure you achieve your aspirations in the shortest period of time and in the most efficient manner. A plan provides a clear sense of direction and defines the components that will support the achievement of your aspirations. Clarify your aspirations by building a personal strategic plan that will help lead you to success.*

CHAPTER 7:
Implement your Strategic Plan

"The only place where success comes before work is in the dictionary."

— Vidal Sassoon

Just as every successful company takes ideas and thoughtfully and skillfully translates them into action, so must you. Any company with groundbreaking ideas that fails to act upon these ideas will not remain in business for very long. Every great idea still requires a plan – and every plan must be implemented if the idea is ever to be realized. No matter how great the idea, it is only just an idea until it is implemented.

You have tremendous reason to be proud. You have created your personal strategic plan! But completing your plan does not mean your work is done. Discipline and commitment are necessary if your strategic plan is to have any true value. The work will not be easy. The effort required to implement your personal strategic plan might turn out to be the most difficult task you have ever undertaken – but it also might turn out to be the most rewarding. Deciding if you are worth the effort is up to you. I believe you are worth it!

Your personal strategic plan was created by you for you. *You* are **accountable** for its ultimate success or failure. In this respect, you are your own CEO. The only person you will let down by failing to implement your strategic plan is *you*. Take responsibility for your own career! You completed the planning portion of your strategic plan in the previous chapters; now it is time to move from the planning phase to the doing phase. It is up to *you* to take action to achieve your aspirations in a **timely** manner.

Successfully beginning and completing the goals and initiatives of your plan is entirely about having the **discipline** and the **will** to complete them on time. This work must remain a constant daily priority for you. There is no room for procrastination. Remember that you are a product. You need to focus on yourself and upgrade yourself by completing your stated initiatives in order to increase your market value.

You've taken the time to align initiatives with goals that support your aspiration. You've created an organized **plan** that will lead to success. You must be prepared to **prioritize** your activities and carve out the time from your busy life that is required to implement your personal strategic plan. If you approach these tasks in an unsystematic and chaotic manner, you will sabotage your efforts.

Sometimes when faced with a new experience, you may hesitate to take that first step which initiates forward movement. This is Cheryl's experience. She feels hesitation in moving beyond her role as an administrative assistant. In her role as a mother and as an assistant, Cheryl had become quite comfortable in taking care of and satisfying the needs and requests of others. She found herself in a new, uncomfortable situation when she began exploring her needs and aspirations and prioritizing them accordingly. Putting her goals, initiatives and aspirations on paper and then acting on them was a new experience for Cheryl.

On a flight during a family vacation, Cheryl listens to the safety instructions for the use of an oxygen mask. Adults on the plane are advised that should the oxygen masks be deployed, they are to secure their own mask first before attempting to help others around them. In an epiphany, Cheryl understands the analogy to her career exploration: she would not be choosing to take care of herself *instead* of others, but choosing to give herself priority, which would enable her to assist others. This realization gives Cheryl the confidence she needs to reprioritize her life and implement her personal strategic plan.

*"I don't know the key to success, but the key
to failure is trying to please everybody."*
– Bill Cosby

Imagine you are sitting in the driver's seat of a car with a roadmap showing the best route to your destination resting in your lap. Wouldn't it be discouraging to realize you don't have the knowledge or the skills to actually drive the car to your destination? Simply having the confidence and the desire to start the engine is not enough. You need to acquire the types of skills necessary to put the vehicle into motion and drive confidently to your destination.

Mackenzie realized she would need to acquire the skills to put her plans in motion and successfully implement her strategic plan. She recognized that by itself, the desire to succeed would not be enough because she lacked key skills. She realized her lack of skills in these key areas would remain a barrier to her advancement. Mackenzie created, as a priority, initiatives that focused on improving her skills in the area of time management and project management.

Successful women demonstrate the willingness to take on new challenges, to work hard and to manage a variety of simultaneous tasks. By focusing on initiatives and action items and by holding yourself accountable, you *can* implement your strategic plan in a timely manner. Completing each initiative will build your confidence and increase your sense of accomplishment.

As you implement your personal strategic plan, here is a list of skills and personal attributes to consider:

- **Ability to Manage Time:** Time management skills are key to being successful in the business world because they help you prioritize your activities. You can accomplish more in a shorter period of time, and the more you can accomplish, the more valuable you will become. Time management will be seen as a key differentiator.

- **Ability to Organize:** Being organized helps conserve both energy and time that can be used to complete your initiatives. Anticipate and plan for disruptions.

- **Ability to Discipline Yourself:** Being disciplined is about being prepared every time in every situation. It's assuring the preparation required for each task is in place.

- **Ability to Hold Yourself Accountable:** By holding yourself accountable, you take control of your life and your career. You are responsible for the choices you make and the rewards you reap.

When I first started using these techniques to improve myself, I found the easiest way to stay organized and manage my time wisely was to use a three-ring notebook binder. I used the binder to store all of the results of my exercises, my personal strategic plan and my resumé. I then kept the binder on my desk so I could pull it open and look at it and revise everything in it on a regular basis.

Keeping everything in a binder also made it easy for me to carry it to and from home and work and to share it with other women and provide them with ideas. And to this day, almost 15 years after I first started this process, I still have a personal development binder on my desk and I still update the contents on a regular basis. I now have a learned behavior that is easy to maintain and I plan to keep learning and improving myself every day of my life.

Another way to help you successfully implement your personal strategic plan is by finding a mentor. First, let's look at the difference between a mentor and a coach. A **mentor** is generally someone farther up the career ladder than you, someone who has experience and knowledge you currently lack. They are someone you admire for their professionalism, for their knowledge and for their ability to succeed in difficult situations. They are politically savvy in business and are admired for their fair treatment of others.

A mentor provides career guidance and can help with career opportunities because they are generally a senior-level manager from within the same company or industry. They act as your advisor and provide suggestions and guidance on development opportunities, career paths, and leadership strategies. A mentor relationship may be formal (arranged between the individuals or with the help of the HR department) or informal. A critical element within a mentoring relationship is mutual respect. A mentor is generally not paid for services.

A **coach** focuses specifically on your personal development and learning. Coaches observe your performance, analyze your skills, behavior and attitude and provide you with an unbiased, outside perspective to help you improve your efficiency and effectiveness. A coach may be a manager or colleague within your company or industry; however, a coach is most commonly someone who is hired by you or hired through your human resources department for a contracted length of time (usually six months to three years) for a specific fee. The coach works with you during the contracted time period on such areas as knowledge transfer/training, behavior modification, behavior modeling, and image enhancement. They may help you develop or enhance a skill set and improve leadership capabilities.

A coach is hired to help you become the best you can be both personally and professionally; in essence, a tutor. Hiring a coach is usually a formal process where the coach and "coachee" agree upon specific coaching goals, discuss and agree on expectations of the relationship (such as confidentiality and safety), agree on how they will communicate and schedule meetings (over the telephone, in person, via email, etc.), agree on how they will measure success and the specific metrics that will be used, agree on the time commitment for the coaching sessions, etc. In a coaching relationship, it is critical for you to be open to having your coach observe your work and for you to be open to feedback. You must also respect your coach. Keep in mind the fact that mentors and coaches do not provide consultative services as licensed mental health professionals and are not intended to replace counseling, therapy or mental health care.

Deciding if you need or want a mentor or a coach is really up to you. Mentors can be incredibly helpful because they can aid you in navigating the often-confusing maze of the business world in your company or industry. A coach will help you accelerate your efficiency and effectiveness; after all, there's a reason why professional athletes use coaches.

Asking someone to be your mentor can be intimidating but is worth the effort. A formal mentoring relationship is usually the best approach, where the two of you agree on the scope of the relationship and the topics for discussion. In general, the mentor and person being mentored agree to a schedule of meetings on a periodic basis. At the beginning of these meetings you agree on the topics to be discussed. The mentor listens and provides guidance, helpful advice and suggestions. It has been my experience that formalized mentoring relationships usually work better because both parties take the relationship very seriously. That's not to say you shouldn't have friends or colleagues with whom you can obtain quick feedback and reality checks.

Your mentor is someone who takes your best interest to heart and is committed to helping you achieve your goals and aspirations. But remember, this is *your* plan. *You* are accountable for your goals, initiatives, dreams and aspirations, not your mentor. *You* are accountable for implementing your plan. *You* are responsible for your career, not your mentor.

Do not look to your mentor to provide solutions to your problems! It is your job to look at situations and analyze them, determine your objectives, understand and seek alternatives and decide on the best choice or direction. Your mentor is there as an objective and experienced observer to help you explore all your options, help you make the most informed decisions, and help you understand obstacles and the ways around them. Your mentor is not there to hand you solutions on a silver platter!

Here are some helpful hints for seeking and approaching a mentor:

- When looking for a mentor, don't restrict yourself. Good mentors can be found in a variety of places such as your current workplace, other companies in your area, non-profit organizations, church groups, community groups such as the chamber of commerce, etc.

- Prior to seeking a mentor, be sure you write down and clarify what your specific expectations are of the mentor and the role you want them to play.

- Once you've identified a potential mentor, ask to meet with them to discuss a potential mentoring relationship. This meeting should take place at their convenience, in a mutually comfortable location, and in a place that allows you to speak in confidence.

- At the meeting, explain that you would like to have them as your mentor and why.

- If the person agrees to be your mentor, ensure you both share the same commitment to your expectations. Be clear on the time required and availability of your mentor. Establish a meeting schedule with topics for discussion.

- If the person cannot be your mentor, gracefully thank them for their time and if possible, try to gain an understanding of why – are they too overloaded with work currently to take on the role of a mentor, are they willing to consider mentoring you in the future, is there someone they recommend you could contact instead?

- Don't be upset if you are turned down. In my career, I've been turned down twice when seeking a mentor. In both cases, the person I had hoped to have as a mentor was male. Both told me they thought it would be inappropriate to be mentoring a female. So, don't get discouraged! Keep looking until you find a mentor you trust and respect.

It does not matter if you experience some difficulty in completing the actions in your personal strategic plan. What matters is that you keep making the attempt, consistently and repeatedly. Often, we learn more from our attempts and our failures than from our successes.

Because your strategic plan is built around *your* aspirations, implementing it is an opportunity to experience life first hand, not second hand, and without regret. Plan to look back over your life and say, "I accomplished more in my life than I ever thought possible!" Make your time count and achieve your dreams.

*"Discipline is just choosing between what
you want now and what you want most."*
– Anonymous

CHAPTER 7:

Strategic Essential

Implement your Strategic Plan: *Strategic plans, like ideas, are effective only if you implement them. You alone are accountable for your success or failure – you are your own CEO. You must combine the determination to succeed with a commitment to prepare yourself to succeed. Don't just survive life; live it to its fullest.*

CHAPTER 8:
Check your Progress

"I am suffocated and lost when I have not the bright feeling of progression."

— Margaret Fuller

A key ingredient to successful execution of a company's strategic plan is careful review and management of the progress of the initiatives. It would be hard to imagine a company that does not regularly review its financial activities and performance against its plan. These reviews help identify any modifications in priorities that are needed in order to implement their objectives on schedule. Businesses have long realized that what gets measured and reviewed gets done.

"If you can't measure it you can't manage it."
– William R. Hewlett

To reach your goals, it is important to do what you planned to do. You accomplish this by establishing a way to review and track the progress against your goals and initiatives. Initiatives should not only be completed, but also completed on time and with the quality you expected.

How can you determine the best means of checking your progress? The process will need to demonstrate when you are on track and when you begin to deviate from your plan. Let's take one of Cheryl's goals as an example.

- **Goal 3**: I will become more adept at leading projects by means of education and on-the-job training to increase my professional visibility and my contribution to the store.
  - **Initiative 3a**: Enroll in and complete a seminar on using Project Management software so I can effectively track projects, resources and initiatives.
  - **Timing**: December
  - **Measurement**: Certificate of completion with a passing grade, "B" or better.

We need to identify ways that Cheryl can monitor her progress as she completes her initiative. She can keep track of the grades she receives on individual assignments and tests throughout the quarter. She can keep a journal where she records examples of her proactive leadership at work. She could also obtain regular feedback from her manager by scheduling and attending monthly appointments.

Now let's take one of Mackenzie's goals and a supporting initiative as an example.

- **Goal 3**: I will overcome my fear of speaking in front of large groups by taking a speech class; I will improve my image; and I will obtain additional on-the-job experience by the end of this year.
  - **Initiative 3d**: Find a personal image consultant to help me improve my overall look to one that is more professional.
  - **Timing**: Immediate.
  - **Measurement**: Receive recommendations from consultant.

Mackenzie can check her progress as she completes her initiative in the following ways:

- Establish a calendar of events that includes:
  - This week: Research potential consultants
  - Next week: Interview and find a consultant
  - Next week: Schedule an initial meeting
  - Over next four weeks: Make appointments based on consultant recommendations: wardrobe review, color consultation and make-up lessons, among others.

As Mackenzie acts on one of her initiatives, she further improves the likelihood of achieving her goal by clarifying the word "immediate". She further defines her expectation as to what benefits will result from her association with the image consultant. *Quick words of note here...* it can be helpful to look for ways to do things without having to spend a lot of money. Many clothing stores offer free services of consultants who can help you create a very professional image and help you with clothing decisions. But keep in mind that their goal is for you to spend money in their store in exchange for the free services.

By going through this process, both Cheryl and Mackenzie are in a position to monitor their progress and take remedial action if required. If Cheryl begins to experience grades below a "B" average, she can take actions to get back on track.

Mackenzie now has a clear plan for completing her initiative. She has created a calendar to follow. Her initiative is no longer just an after thought but a commitment built into her daily calendar. This gives the initiative the priority and focus necessary to be successfully completed in the shortest period of time possible.

As you monitor the progress of your personal strategic plan, here is a list of helpful hints:

- Review progress on a regular schedule. Get into the habit of setting aside personal time to review your progress. Give yourself the luxury of spending time working on and thinking about you!

- When reviewing each initiative, think of ways to track the progress toward completing the initiative. Remember that quality counts; don't compromise on quality!

- Checking your progress is about more than just checking the box for completion. It is very important to apply the skills and knowledge you've learned through your reading, classes, seminars, etc. Unapplied learning is quickly forgotten, while learning when applied to actual work experience is re-enforced and strengthened.

- Time management tools can greatly increase your success in managing your progress. Tools such as personal data assistants (PDAs) may be purchased with software that allows calendar functions (you can easily enter your information electronically and then print it out). Hard copy day planners are available in most office supply stores.

- "Go ugly early." This means that you should take immediate corrective action to unproductive plans as they become apparent. Do not procrastinate!

- Regularly update your resumé. Every time you complete a class, seminar or training program, immediately update your resumé with this information. Always keep copies of your updated resumé with you, even on vacations and business trips. It can be invaluable to have an updated resumé at your fingertips! I have been offered jobs many times while flying on airplanes, while at conferences, and during trade shows.

- Keep a list of the titles and authors of all the books you read each year. When interviewing, it is helpful to use this list to demonstrate your proactive efforts to improve your knowledge on an on-going basis. One of the questions I always ask when I'm interviewing job applicants is, "Tell me about the books you've read over the last 12 months." I ask this question because I'm looking for candidates who actively seek to improve their knowledge on an on-going basis. I don't want to hire people who stop learning once they're out of school.

- After you have completed a goal, check to see if it's the right time for you to take on a new one.

Checking your progress provides you with the opportunity to identify, early on, obstacles in achieving your initiatives and ultimate goals. Once aware of identified problems, you are in a better position to take immediate action. Without this information, you could find yourself so far behind you might be tempted to abandon important goals you set for yourself.

Regular review and documentation of your progress will result in a disciplined approach to managing even the most complex personal strategic plan. You are worth the time and effort that it takes!

"Energy is the essence of life.
Every day you decide how you're going to
use it by knowing what you want and
what it takes to reach that goal,
and by maintaining focus."
– Oprah Winfrey

CHAPTER 8:

Strategic Essential

Check your Progress: *Having and implementing a strategic plan requires that you review and demonstrate progress in order to take corrective action. Make immediate corrections to unproductive or unsuccessful plans as soon as they become apparent. Do not procrastinate!*

CHAPTER 9:
Stay Focused

"There are people who put their dreams in a little box and say, 'Yes, I've got dreams, of course, I've got dreams.' Then they put the box away and bring it out once in a while to look in it, and yep, they're still there. These are great dreams, but they never even get out of the box. It takes an uncommon amount of guts to put your dreams on the line, to hold them up and say, 'How good or how bad am I?' That's where courage comes in."
— Erma Bombeck

Your personal strategic plan represents your aspirations. Are you now going to put it in a drawer and forget about it, bringing it out only now and again to admire it? You may be feeling such a sense of relief and accomplishment at this point that you fail to complete the implementation of your strategic plan.

You may offer many reasons for putting your strategic plan aside: you are caught up in your work life, your personal life, and your family's activities. Excuses may come easily now. Do not become a victim of procrastination! Not completing the work you have begun should be unacceptable to you. Finish what you have begun. Your work life, personal life, and family life will benefit from your focus and making your aspirations a reality.

Staying focused is up to you. No one can achieve your dreams for you; that responsibility is yours alone. Only your tenacity, your energy, and your personal commitment are required.

As you begin to implement your plan, you may find that the work is hard and that staying focused is lonely. As you achieve milestones, your resolution will bring a sense of renewal and motivation. You will begin to see a return on your investment – your energy will be replenished, providing you with the inspiration to continue.

"There is no such thing as can't, only won't.
If you're qualified, all it takes is a burning desire
to accomplish, to make a change.
Go forward, go backward. Whatever it takes!
But you can't blame other people or society in general.
It all comes from your mind. When we do the impossible
we realize we are special people."
– Jan Ashford

Unfortunately, sooner or later, others will seek to sabotage your efforts. All of us have experienced occasions when we have been the targets of cutting remarks disguised as praise or hollow-sounding encouragement. As you enjoy increased success, anticipate sabotage.

As you gain more competence and momentum in your career, you will encounter people who are threatened by your sense of self-confidence. They will see you achieving more and taking on more responsibility – and will fear that your success will come at their expense. Without exploring the psychology of their behavior, I guarantee that sabotage will happen. It will happen regardless of your behavior.

I encountered sabotage at the beginning of my career. I was working for a large company and my supervisor went out on maternity leave. Upon her departure, I was promoted, on an interim basis, to 'acting supervisor'. This gave me the opportunity to broaden my experience and ensure the department continued to run smoothly until she returned. Upon her return, she became hostile and downright deceitful in her behavior towards me – to the point that she even resorted to sabotaging my work in order to make me look bad to the department director.

After directly approaching her to try to understand her behavior, I came to realize she was simply jealous of me. During my time as acting supervisor I had made many changes in the department that had positively impacted productivity, quality and morale. She wrongly assumed I was out to gain her job and therefore saw me as her enemy. Don't let the bad behavior of others keep you from pursuing your aspirations. The key to dealing with saboteurs is preparing for them.

Effie H. Jones once said, "Failing to plan is a plan to fail." As you prepare yourself to deal with these types of situations, I offer the following suggestions:

- Always remain confident in your skills and abilities. Don't allow others to undermine your belief in yourself.

- Regularly review your strategic plan and the value of the aspirations you are pursuing. Remain true to your mission.

- Business can sometimes become very personal. Always try to see situations from an unemotional point of view, considering all perspectives.

- Never be afraid to approach someone directly when negative situations arise. Be bold, be brave and sit down privately with the person to talk about the situation.

- Remember that you simply cannot please everyone. Stay true to yourself.

The achievement of your aspirations should be more important than any discomfort, sadness, confusion, or loneliness you may temporarily experience at the hands of others. Too many people allow others to stand in their way or negatively influence their ability to pursue their strategic plan. Remember, what is best is not always easiest. You are special and can achieve the impossible through tenacity, commitment and belief in yourself.

> *"It is a bad plan that admits of no modification."*
> – Publilius Syrus, Moral Sayings, 1st century B.C.

The world is not a perfect place and no plan is perfect or achieved in a vacuum. All plans continue to be influenced by external factors and new information. The trick is to be flexible enough to analyze the factors influencing your plan and adjust or modify accordingly. It would be unrealistic to imagine a plan that needs no modification or adjustment while maintaining the integrity of the goal. You must be able to make adjustments without losing sight of your aspiration.

Before modifying your goal, though, make sure a need for modification exists. You may find you need to re-double your efforts and increase your focus to get yourself back on track, rather than adjust your goal. Don't confuse the need to modify with the natural consequences of procrastinating.

Let's return to Cheryl and Mackenzie and observe their progress. Cheryl enrolls in a speech class and purchases several books on communications. She enters her first class excited and enthusiastic. She soon realizes that the class requires a much greater time commitment than she had anticipated. In reviewing her progress and her goal of achieving a grade of B or better, she determines that she needs to be more disciplined in setting aside time to prepare for her class. Nevertheless, her first test result is a C. She also has not begun to read any of her communications books. She is faced with the choice of dropping out of class or being willing to accept a lower grade. Cheryl is willing to do neither.

She reflects on the root cause of the problems she is having keeping up with her speech class. What she finds is the time she intends to spend studying in the evening is being repeatedly interrupted by unscheduled social emergencies with her family. Too often one of her children would declare that a school project demands her last minute help; cookies need to be baked for a school fundraiser or a driver is needed for taking the children to activities outside of school. She decides to devise a plan that allows more time for homework so she can catch up in class, achieve her goal of a B average, and read her communications books. Cheryl decides to speak with her family and ask for their support in proactively planning and managing their activities. She realizes their cooperation would minimize the emergencies that have been disrupting the time she plans to devote to schoolwork and reading.

Three weeks later, Cheryl receives the results of her last speech assignment and test. She has improved her grade to a B-. She has also finished reading her first communications book. Now that her family understands the importance she places on completing her initiatives regarding schoolwork, Cheryl feels much less stress. Her sons see Cheryl working on assignments in the evening and are studying harder themselves, trying to "be like Mom."

Mackenzie's quest to achieve her aspiration of becoming a vice president of marketing as soon as possible leads her to focus on multiple initiatives in addition to enrolling in classes. In reviewing her progress, she finds that, although she is off to a quick start in school, she is unable to consistently attend and participate in Toastmasters. She realizes that, once again, she has taken on more than she can handle and is risking her credibility by being unable to fulfill her well-intended commitments.

After reviewing her schedule and activities both at work and at home, Mackenzie decides she is not willing to compromise her time and effort on the job. While Toastmasters is valuable to her long-term goal, she nevertheless contacts them to explain her decision to postpone participation to a later date. She is assured her involvement would be welcomed in the future as her schedule allows.

In both cases, Cheryl and Mackenzie were able to identify and resolve problems early and take decisive corrective action without abandoning their commitments to themselves. They did not put their dreams on hold; they had the courage to confront and resolve problems.

Maintaining your focus and commitment to implement your personal strategic plan will have its challenges. Using techniques to monitor your progress, you can prepare yourself to face those challenges and address them head on. Modifications can be made without compromising the integrity of your plan. A positive attitude, combined with a process of reviewing, assessing and modifying when necessary, will help assure your ultimate success. Never put your dreams in a box, hiding them from the light of day. Have the courage to act on them and the tenacity to accomplish them.

> *"The only thing that separates successful people*
> *from the ones who aren't is the*
> *willingness to work very, very hard."*
> – Helen Gurley Brown

CHAPTER 9:

Strategic Essential

Stay Focused: *Tenacity, courage and commitment are essential to achieving your aspirations. Staying focused is up to you. Only you can achieve your dreams. Focus on the positive, but be prepared to overcome obstacles. Be aware that all plans, at some point, may need to be modified.*

CHAPTER 10:
Celebrate and Reward Achievements

"In every work / a reward added makes the pleasure twice as great."

— Euripides

Congratulations! Fantastic job! Excellent work! I really appreciate what you're doing! How did you feel right now when you read that? Would you like to hear those words again? *Congratulations! Fantastic job! Excellent work! I really appreciate what you're doing!* Doesn't it feel great to have someone acknowledge all the hard work you've done in creating and implementing your personal strategic plan? Does hearing those words of encouragement provide you with motivation to complete what you have begun?

Receiving positive recognition provides motivation to continue achieving initiatives. So often we get caught up in the daily demands of our work and personal lives that we forget to reward ourselves when we achieve milestones. We do the hard work, but we don't take the opportunity to reap the benefits and pleasure derived from taking a moment to celebrate. You should celebrate and reward your achievements so you can supercharge yourself through the completion of your personal strategic plan.

You can't count on someone else to pat you on the back or provide you with timely feedback. So, don't wait for others to acknowledge your effort and achievement. You need to be your own coach, your own manager, your own cheerleader; and you need to give yourself those well-deserved words of encouragement. Your approval is what matters.

Make sure your manager knows about all the incredible things you are doing and that those items get noted in your performance appraisal. You should regularly sit down with your manager to review your projects and what you are accomplishing.

If you currently work somewhere where you haven't been given a performance appraisal, write your own self-evaluation and provide it to your manager to add their comments. Then, keep a copy for yourself and submit a copy to the human resources department to include in your personnel file.

You need to establish what accomplishments in your personal strategic plan are worth celebrating, set the criteria for what merits a reward celebration, and then celebrate! Your criteria may include the following:

- Completing an initiative, such as finishing a seminar or class while achieving your goal grade.
- Completing a mid-term test successfully.
- Completing a book on time.
- Showing up the first time to a new class, course, or seminar. Showing up the last day of a class.
- Recognizing a positive change or a successful performance.

But remember that you must have earned the reward. Don't reward yourself for procrastinating; don't pat yourself on the back for completing a project or accomplishing a goal at the last minute. Establish standards that make you proud and represent the high expectation you've set for yourself through your personal strategic plan.

Celebrations and rewards come in all sizes and flavors. Be creative and have fun! The rewards need not be lavish; they only need to please *you*. Here are some suggestions:

- Treat yourself and a friend to coffee before work.
- Buy a bouquet of your favorite flowers and put them on your desk at work. Every time you glance at your flowers, you will be reminded of what you accomplished.
- Give yourself a day off to play, relax at home watching your favorite movies or go explore an art gallery.
- Go to lunch at your favorite restaurant with a colleague or friend.
- Go out to a movie with your friends or invite them over to watch a movie and eat popcorn.
- Go to dinner with someone special or treat yourself by making your favorite meal while sipping a glass of wine.
- Buy tickets for a special evening at the symphony, opera, theater, or a sporting event.
- Buy yourself new clothes – a new outfit or a single item (sweater, piece of jewelry).
- Treat yourself to a manicure or pedicure.
- Plan a weekend getaway to somewhere you've never been and then go exploring.
- Take your family to a zoo, aquarium, or museum.

A great way to get into the habit of celebrating and rewarding yourself is to buy a journal (or use the included template and keep them in your three-ring binder for inspiration) and record your accomplishments, the way you feel, and the reward you gave yourself. Share your accomplishments with your family or friends. Here is a sample journal entry:

March 11th: Completed the final exam in my speech class this quarter and earned an A. Felt like I could fly home from class that night. The entire family celebrated by taking me out for a banana split and a movie on Saturday.

_____'s List of Accomplishments:

DATE	ACCOMPLISHMENT	HOW I REWARDED MYSELF

Success is not a by-product of luck. Success is the result of careful planning, work, and effort. You worked hard to understand yourself, your assets and liabilities, your differentiators, external perceptions, your competitors, your goals – you created and implemented your strategic plan, you evaluated your progress. You have worked hard to achieve your goals and aspirations, so take pride in yourself and celebrate your achievements! Do not deflect attention from yourself. Abandon thoughts of shunning recognition or shifting credit to others. Enjoy the spotlight!

Let's check back in with Cheryl and Mackenzie to see how they've been celebrating and rewarding their accomplishments. Cheryl recently enrolled in a two-day seminar on "Finance for the Non-Financial Manager." When the day arrives, she is a bit hesitant and nervous at first, remembering that math is not her best subject and fearful she will say something foolish. At the seminar, she is surrounded by people she doesn't know, increasing her doubts about attending. But what she discovers is just how much she already knows about the practical application of finance. Her experience at work has already given her considerable applicable knowledge and reinforces her confidence that she can handle and benefit from the seminar. Further, she is able to build on her knowledge and learn new concepts and information.

When Cheryl completes the seminar she feels proud of herself and secure in the new skills she has learned. She writes the following entry in her journal:

"Today I completed what I thought would be one of my most difficult challenges. I not only successfully completed "Finance for the Non-Financial Manager" but I also met people I consider new friends. Bob and I have decided to celebrate with a night of dinner and dancing next weekend. I deserve it!"

Since completing her finance course, Cheryl's manager has given her the permanent assignment of monitoring the department's expenses against their budget. Her manager not only recognizes that Cheryl successfully completed the seminar, but also that she has more confidence in handling new assignments.

Mackenzie has been working to complete a speech class. Much to her surprise, after overcoming her initial fear of speaking in front of the class, she discovers that she really enjoys public speaking. Upon completion of her class she treats herself with a shopping spree to buy a new power suit.

Mackenzie feels excited and energized as she shops for her new suit. She challenged herself with a class and she successfully stuck to it and completed it. She is no longer terrified at the thought of speaking before a large group of people; she now feels confident and in control. Within a month, Mackenzie receives an opportunity from her manager to provide training during an upcoming meeting. Not only does she put together a creative presentation, she delivers it with poise and panache! Her efforts result in many compliments from the participants, who assure her that it was one of the best training sessions they have ever attended. Mackenzie, by the way, looked terrific in her new suit.

Both Cheryl and Mackenzie are well on their way to achieving their aspirations. They have gone beyond simply wishing something better would happen to them to making it happen through planning, hard work and actions. They have achieved happier, fuller lives as a result of their efforts to take control of their careers and improve themselves.

"Happiness is not a goal, it is a by-product."
– Eleanor Roosevelt

You too can be a Cheryl or a Mackenzie. You can manage your career, *your* way. You can put yourself in the driver's seat, steering yourself toward destinations of *your* choice. So make the commitment to treat yourself like a product, to continually upgrade yourself, and differentiate yourself from others. You *can* do it; I believe in you. Now, believe in yourself. Take control and be proactive! Success and happiness will be your reward. Never doubt that your dreams are worthy of your best efforts. The work is hard but you're worth the investment!

"What really matters is what you do with what you have."
– Shirley Lord

CHAPTER 10:

Strategic Essential

Celebrate and Reward Achievements: *Giving yourself encouragement and rewards will provide motivation and pleasure as you continue achieving your goals. You cannot count on others to shine a spotlight on you. You must be your own coach / manager.*

GO CELEBRATE!

The 10 Personal Strategic Essentials

Review your Assets and Liabilities

Remind yourself that you are valuable and that you possess strengths. Define yourself as a competitive product. Challenge yourself by facing any weaknesses and commit yourself to systematic improvement and upgrades.

Determine your Differentiators

Just as products have strengths that set them apart, so do people. A differentiator is a competitive advantage. Identify those things that you do better than other people. Your distinctive strengths are what others perceive your value to be.

Obtain Customer Feedback

Perception is reality. Seek to understand the perception others have of you. With this knowledge you can be confident of your assessment of your assets, liabilities and differentiators. If you find that a change needs to be made, you are then in a better position to focus your time and efforts to make this happen.

Identify and Evaluate your Competitors

Competition is a fact of life. Simply doing your job and hoping for the best is not enough. You need to compete for what you want. Competition and what you can learn from it should be viewed positively and embraced. Strive to be your best by understanding yourself and your competitors.

Determine your Goals

Goals reflect what you want to accomplish to improve yourself. They are your targets, both short-term and long-term. Goal setting will lead you to a greater sense of commitment and motivation as you pursue your aspirations.

Create your Strategic Plan

Like using a roadmap to arrive at a destination, having a clear plan in place helps assure you achieve your aspirations in the shortest period of time and in the most efficient manner. A plan provides a clear sense of direction and defines the components that will support the achievement of your aspirations. Clarify your aspirations by building a personal strategic plan that will help lead you to success.

Implement your Strategic Plan

Strategic plans, like ideas, are effective only if you implement them. You alone are accountable for your success or failure – you are your own CEO. You must combine the determination to succeed with a commitment to prepare yourself to succeed. Don't just survive life; live it to its fullest.

Check your Progress

Having and implementing a strategic plan requires that you review and demonstrate progress in order to take corrective action. Make immediate corrections to unproductive or unsuccessful plans as soon as they become apparent. Do not procrastinate!

Stay Focused

Tenacity, courage and commitment are essential to achieving your aspirations. Staying focused is up to you. Only you can achieve your dreams. Focus on the positive, but be prepared to overcome obstacles. Be aware that all plans, at some point, may need to be modified.

Celebrate and Reward Achievements

Giving yourself encouragement and rewards will provide motivation and pleasure as you continue achieving your goals. You cannot count on others to shine a spotlight on you. You must be your own coach / manager.

Appendix A: Templates

To assist you in completing the exercises, all templates are available electronically to download. Just go to the website, **www.careerwomaninc.com** and from the Home Page, click on "**Resources**" – then look for this book and you may download the templates after you enter the password, "**Athena**".

_____'s List of Assets and Liabilities:

ASSETS	LIABILITIES
• _____	• _____
_____	_____
• _____	• _____
_____	_____
• _____	• _____
_____	_____
• _____	• _____
_____	_____
• _____	• _____
_____	_____
• _____	• _____
_____	_____
• _____	• _____
_____	_____

_____'s *List of Admired People:*

NAME	KEY ASSET / DIFFERENTIATOR

_____'s List of Assets:

ORIGINAL LIST	PRIORITIZED LIST	DIFFERENTIATOR
	1.	
	2.	
	3.	
	4.	
	5.	
	6.	
	7.	
	8.	
	9.	
	10.	

Reminder: Draw a circle around your top three assets.

Feedback From: _____

ASSETS	IMPROVEMENT OPPORTUNITIES

Feedback From: _____

ASSETS	IMPROVEMENT OPPORTUNITIES

Feedback From: _____

ASSETS	IMPROVEMENT OPPORTUNITIES

Requirements for _____ position:

REQUIREMENTS
1.
2.
3.
4.
5.
6.
7.
8.
9.
10.

_____'s Competitive Analysis:

REQUIREMENTS	YOUR NAME	COMPETITOR	COMPETITOR	COMPETITOR
Current Position				
Key Strengths				
Key Weaknesses				

_____'s S.W.O.T. Analysis:

STRENGTHS (ASSETS)	WEAKNESSES (LIABILITIES)
• _____	• _____
• _____	• _____
• _____	• _____
• _____	• _____
• _____	• _____
• _____	• _____

THREATS (COMPETITOR STRENGTHS)	OPPORTUNITIES (INITIATIVES)
• _____	• _____
• _____	• _____
• _____	• _____
• _____	• _____
• _____	• _____
• _____	• _____

_____'s *List of Goals:*

GOALS	INITIATIVES	TIMING

_____'s Strategic Plan:

ASPIRATION	GOALS	INITIATIVES	TIMING	MEASUREMENT	STATUS
ASSETS					
LIABILITIES					
DIFFERENTIATORS					
THREATS					

_____'s *List of Accomplishments:*

DATE	ACCOMPLISHMENT	HOW I REWARDED MYSELF

The 10 Personal Strategic Essentials

Review your Assets and Liabilities

Remind yourself that you are valuable and that you possess strengths. Define yourself as a competitive product. Challenge yourself by facing any weaknesses and commit yourself to systematic improvement and upgrades.

Determine your Differentiators

Just as products have strengths that set them apart, so do people. A differentiator is a competitive advantage. Identify those things that you do better than other people. Your distinctive strengths are what others perceive your value to be.

Obtain Customer Feedback

Perception is reality. Seek to understand the perception others have of you. With this knowledge you can be confident of your assessment of your assets, liabilities and differentiators. If you find that a change needs to be made, you are then in a better position to focus your time and efforts to make this happen.

Identify and Evaluate your Competitors

Competition is a fact of life. Simply doing your job and hoping for the best is not enough. You need to compete for what you want. Competition and what you can learn from it should be viewed positively and embraced. Strive to be your best by understanding yourself and your competitors.

Determine your Goals

Goals reflect what you want to accomplish to improve yourself. They are your targets, both short-term and long-term. Goal setting will lead you to a greater sense of commitment and motivation as you pursue your aspirations.

Create your Strategic Plan

Like using a roadmap to arrive at a destination, having a clear plan in place helps assure you achieve your aspirations in the shortest period of time and in the most efficient manner. A plan provides a clear sense of direction and defines the components that will support the achievement of your aspirations. Clarify your aspirations by building a personal strategic plan that will help lead you to success.

Implement your Strategic Plan

Strategic plans, like ideas, are effective only if you implement them. You alone are accountable for your success or failure – you are your own CEO. You must combine the determination to succeed with a commitment to prepare yourself to succeed. Don't just survive life; live it to its fullest.

Check your Progress

Having and implementing a strategic plan requires that you review and demonstrate progress in order to take corrective action. Make immediate corrections to unproductive or unsuccessful plans as soon as they become apparent. Do not procrastinate!

Stay Focused

Tenacity, courage and commitment are essential to achieving your aspirations. Staying focused is up to you. Only you can achieve your dreams. Focus on the positive, but be prepared to overcome obstacles. Be aware that all plans, at some point, may need to be modified.

Celebrate and Reward Achievements

Giving yourself encouragement and rewards will provide motivation and pleasure as you continue achieving your goals. You cannot count on others to shine a spotlight on you. You must be your own coach / manager.

I Want To Hear From You

I want to hear how this book has changed, helped or inspired you. How have you applied your newly found knowledge to progress in your career? Has this book helped you take on a new challenge in your career? If so, how did it help you? Has it helped you accomplish anything that had previously been out of your reach? Tell me about that. Visit **www.careerwomaninc.com** and share your success stories and experiences.

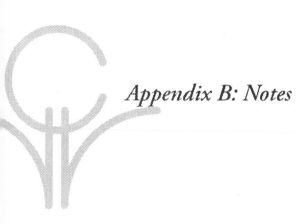

Appendix B: Notes

Notes

Notes

Notes

Notes

Notes

Notes

Notes

Notes

Index

Quotation Biographical Index

A

Arland, Gilbert, *64*
(b. not available)
Writer

Ash, Mary Kay, *56*
(1915-2001)
American businesswoman

Ashford, Jan, *92*
(b. 1932)
American businesswoman

B

Berger, Sally, *14*
(b. 1933)
American businesswoman

Bombeck, Erma, *91*
(1927-1996)
American humorist

Brown, Helen Gurley, *95*
(b. 1922)
American publisher, author

C

Clark, Karen Kaiser, *1*
(b. 1938)
American state legislator, lecturer,
author, consultant, educator, feminist

Cosby, Bill, *78*
(b. 1937)
American television personality,
movie actor

D

De Saint-Exupery, Antoine, *53*
(1900-1944)
French writer

Du Deffand, Marquise, *65*
(1697-1780)
French society intellectual

DiSesa, Nina, *56*
(b. not available)
American businesswoman

E

Evert, Chris, *35*
(b. 1954)
American tennis champion

Euripides, *97*
(~480 BC-406 BC)
Greek poet

F

Fuller, Margaret, *85*
(1810-1850)
American writer

H

Hazlitt, William, *15*
(1778-1830)
English writer

Hewlett, William R., *85*
(1913-2001)
American businessman, inventor

Holmes, Oliver Wendell Sr., *25*
(1809-1894)
American physician, professor, writer

J

Jones, Effie H., *93*
(b. 1928)
*American association executive,
educator*

L

Lord, Shirley, *103*
(b. not available)
American writer, magazine editor

M

Margrethe II, *5*
(b. 1940)
Queen of Denmark

N

Naso, Publius Ovidius, *37*
(43 BC-17 CE)
Roman poet

R

Roosevelt, Eleanor, *4, 34, 102*
(1884-1962)
*American First Lady, humanitarian,
U.N. Delegate*

S

Sassoon, Vidal, *77*
(b. 1928)
World-renowned hair stylist

Sawyer, Diane, *52*
(b. 1945)
American broadcast journalist

Syrus, Publilius, *93*
(~1st century BC)
Latin writer of mimes

T

Thatcher, Margaret, *7*
(b. 1925)
First female British prime minister

W

Walters, Barbara, *23*
(b. 1931)
American broadcast journalist

Washington, Martha, *13*
(1732-1802)
American First Lady

Winfrey, Oprah, *57, 89*
(b. 1954)
*American businesswoman,
television personality, movie actress*

About the Author

LISA QUAST

Lisa Quast has succeeded at business and in her career in areas that have been traditionally male dominated. She has extensive experience in the global high technology healthcare industry in the areas of strategic planning, business development, marketing, sales, service, and operations. She is recognized for the successful development of personnel and organizations and is well known for her executive coaching and mentoring services. Lisa is the President of Career Woman, Inc., is a sought after speaker and executive coach, earned the 2006 Woman of the Year Award from the American Biographical Institute, and was named by the *Puget Sound Business Journal* as one of the top 40 business leaders in Seattle. The award honors top leaders under the age of 40 who work hard to drive the business community's future and demonstrate dynamic leadership and social responsibility.

Dear Readers,

If you're motivated to help yourself and also help others after reading this book, please consider supporting Dress for Success®.

The mission of Dress for Success is to promote the economic independence of disadvantaged woman by providing professional attire, a network of support and the career development tools to help women thrive in work and in life.

Dress for Success is a not-for-profit organization that offers services to help women enter the workforce and stay employed. Each dress for Success client receives one suit when she has a job interview and up to a week's worth of separates when she gets the job. The Dress for Success Professional Women's Group program then provides ongoing support to help the client build a successful career.

Dress for Success relies on the support of people who are committed to helping low-income women take charge of their lives. It's easy, and incredibly rewarding, to get involved and make a difference.

For information on how you can help make a difference, please log onto the Dress for Success web site at: www.dressforsuccess.org.

Sincerely,
Lisa Quast

CPSIA information can be obtained at www.ICGtesting.com
261037BV00002B/28/A